INTRODUCING SCIENCE
COMMUNICATION

INTRODUCING SCIENCE COMMUNICATION

A PRACTICAL GUIDE

Edited by
Mark L. Brake
University of Glamorgan, UK
and
Emma Weitkamp
University of West of England, UK

First published 2010 by
PALGRAVE MACMILLAN

Palgrave Macmillan in the UK is an imprint of Macmillan Publishers Limited, registered in England, company number 785998, of Houndmills, Basingstoke, Hampshire RG21 6XS.

Palgrave Macmillan in the US is a division of St Martin's Press LLC, 175 Fifth Avenue, New York, NY 10010.

Palgrave Macmillan is the global academic imprint of the above companies and has companies and representatives throughout the world.

Palgrave® and Macmillan® are registered trademarks in the United States, the United Kingdom, Europe and other countries.

ISBN: 978–0–230–57385–7 hardback
ISBN: 978–0–230–57386–4 paperback

This book is printed on paper suitable for recycling and made from fully managed and sustained forest sources. Logging, pulping and manufacturing processes are expected to conform to the environmental regulations of the country of origin.

A catalogue record for this book is available from the British Library.

A catalog record for this book is available from the Library of Congress.

10 9 8 7 6 5 4 3 2 1
19 18 17 16 15 14 13 12 11 10

Printed in Great Britain by
CPI Antony Rowe, Chippenham and Eastbourne

ers traveling on a particular tour are the same ones who appeared on the group's hit albums or Simon's *Rhythm of the Saints*, and he just laughs.

"Listen," he says, "Olodum always gives opportunity to new musicians. They belong to the social project. They are street children, and enter Olodum when they are like eight, ten, eleven, twelve years old, and they are in Olodum like fifteen years, twelve years, ten years, six years."

So what exactly is Olodum? There does not seem to be a single answer. It is a band, a Carnaval "school" (the groups that march competitively in the Carnaval parades), an Afro-Brazilian cultural center that has classes in everything from music and dance to computer skills, a crafts factory and store, and a political pressure group pushing for black pride and consciousness. The group's website mixes concert reviews and cultural manifestos, and has as much to say about Malcolm X as about music.

All of which does not keep it from being a very hot dance band. Along with Jackson and Simon, Olodum has played with David Byrne, Tracy Chapman, Jimmy Cliff, Herbie Hancock, and Sadao Watanabe, as well as getting several huge hits in Brazil and being voted Bahia's top Carnaval group. Indeed, Olodum's previous musical director, Neguinho do Samba, created the dominant pop style in modern Bahian music, the fusion known as samba reggae.

"Samba is a traditional African music," Arquimimo says. "And it is the rhythm of all Brazil. In 1986, we mixed in the beat of reggae, so you get a new stuff, and also we play other rhythms like *aluja* [a rhythm used in Afro-Brazilian religious ceremonies], merengue, salsa—but the beat, the rhythm is called samba reggae. And now all the groups play it. Olodum itself is invited by singers like Gilberto Gil, Caetano Veloso, and the others . . . what can I say, I forgot all the names."

While their rhythms get the crowd up and dancing—whether in a foreign concert hall or from the roofs of the huge *tríos elétricos*, the mammoth sound trucks of Salvador's Carnaval—Olodum's lyrics often reflect the group's larger concerns. "We talk about many things," Arquimimo says. "We're talking about love, we're talking about social situations. We're talking about the poverty, about the big cities, and about the desert where we don't have the conditions to survive, so people leave their hometown and go to the main center. And we're talking about the racism problem that we face everywhere."

After more than two decades of struggle, Arquimimo feels that Olodum has had a noticeable effect on the surrounding society. "Because of our aim many things have changed," he says. "We have other social groups nowadays in Brazil, and Olodum is like a mirror for many other organizations. This year, we were invited to start a new work in São Paulo with street children and people who live with high risk situations like drugs. They really like the idea of Olodum, how we go with music, with drums, you know, and try to turn the mind of people."

Daniela Mercury

While a handful of Brazilian stars have been highly visible on the world market, they present a very limited picture of the country's music. Brazil not only has many regional folk styles, but it has also produced huge waves of pop music that for one reason or another have failed to reach a non-Brazilian audience. In the United States, the result is that there are two quite separate Brazilian scenes, one crossing over to non-Brazilians and the other only heard by Brazilian students and immigrants. The Brazilian-for-the-Brazilians offerings have included disco-style bands like E o Tchan and the country-and-western fusion called *serteneja*, which clearly would have little appeal to a world audience, but also some artists who would seem like naturals on any stage. Daniela Mercury, for example, has made little impact outside the immigrant community, though she should have been able to cross over like crazy. Onstage, Mercury comes on like the Madonna of Brazilian roots music, performing intricate, impossibly fast choreography along with her back-up dancers while singing catchy, exuberant vocals over an unrelentingly propulsive rhythm section.

It is no surprise to learn that Mercury started out as a dancer. By 1990, though, she was being hailed as the hottest Carnaval singer in Bahia, and queen of the tríos elétricos. Her early work was based on the local *axé* rhythms, mixed with the new samba-reggae fusion.

"I became interested in samba reggae because I thought it was an extremely pop rhythm, very capable of making absolutely everyone dance," Mercury says.* "So I decided to start using it as a base and then introduce electric instruments and harmonizations influenced by MPB, with great musicians from jazz and other genres of Brazilian and international music."

Mercury's greatest album, *Feijao com Arroz* (Beans and Rice), marked an ambitious expansion of her earlier explorations while remaining irresistibly danceable. "It is a more sophisticated recording," she says. "It's a new style, an artistic work that looks to explore and experiment with other musicians along with my musicians. My first albums are more linked to Carnaval. This album is more romantic; it has songs that speak of other themes as well. It has more slow songs, too, and more complex arrangements. We used wind instruments and lots of percussion. I always try to work with different rhythms—that's why it is called *Feijao com Arroz*. This is a traditional dish in Brazil and each region has a different sauce."

The title is also a metaphor for the mix of black and white, and the striking cover photo shows Mercury, with her long reddish hair, hugging a very dark Afro-Brazilian woman. "This embrace symbolizes the beauty of differences," she says. "In Brazil we have a great mix of skin colors, rhythms, influences that make up the Brazilian culture. I believe that differences are what make the world rich. They need to be respected and incorporated so that we can become richer and more creative culturally."

Despite the seriousness of intent, Mercury's new album is, if anything, even more instantly accessible than her more pop-oriented recordings. It starts with a lovely a cappella vocal that flows into lilting reggae, and then fires up the energy on the second track, "Rapunzel," as a screaming electric guitar introduces a merengue-flavored horn section, and then a perky sing-along hook.

Above all, it makes you want to dance. Trained as a modern dancer, Mercury describes her body as "my first instrument," and she remains true to her roots. "I like to mix our street dance, the spontaneous movements of our people, samba, a sensual dance,

---

* This interview was conducted through a translator.

with formal choreography," she says. "I thought about this a lot, and I toured before with even more complex dance choreography, but then I decided to make the dance reflect the music more, to understand the rhythms better through body movements. Because dancing was my first way of feeling music, and I try to pass this on with the work I do onstage. So this way people can feel the meaning of the rhythm."

Though she got her professional start as a nightclub singer, performing the slow, romantic songs of artists like Chico Buarque, Tom Jobim, and Caetano Veloso, Mercury's career took off only after she began dancing and singing on the tríos elétricos, which she describes as "like a concert for two million people, more or less, who are in the streets of Bahia in the spirit of Carnaval." In 1992, an afternoon show in the plaza of the São Paolo Art Museum proved that her appeal was not limited to Bahia, when the overflow crowd stopped traffic for several hours. "I was reviewed in all the newspapers and no one knew where I came from," she recalls with glee. "The headlines were 'Singer from Bahia Stops São Paolo!' After that, everyone was curious to know who I was."

Mercury signed with the Brazilian branch of Sony, and her vibrant new sound was an immediate national sensation. Over her next several albums, she expanded both her vocal abilities and her musical range, adding acoustic instruments to the synthesizers and drum programming of her early work, and seeking out composers and arrangers who suited her style. More than just a dynamic front woman, she has written many of her own tunes and done much of the arranging herself.

In the process of broadening her sound, Mercury has found an audience far beyond Brazil. Her second album earned a gold record in Argentina, though she had not yet appeared there, and she has toured widely in the Americas, Asia, and Europe. A recent album even includes a samba sung in Japanese.

"I feel that this music has no customs controls," Mercury says. "In Germany, Switzerland, France, and Italy, people—without knowing exactly what to do—danced. I am always very interested in the audience. I teach people from the stage some dances. This music has a magic way of communicating. It has a strong force because it is music of the street, like your rap in America, but it's not protest music. It makes people dance and brings a happiness that is the spirit of our people."

Mexico

Los Tigres del Norte

As befits its geographical situation, Mexican music is by far the best-selling Latin style in the United States, but its listenership is almost entirely limited to people whose backgrounds are Mexican or Central American. Anglos have provided a cult audience for Tex-Mex or *conjunto* music—essentially the style that Mexicans call *norteño* (northern)—but the most famous and influential Mexican bands are virtually unknown outside immigrant communities. Los Tigres del Norte, for example, have been the most important band in norteño for over thirty years, and pack huge halls from Los Angeles to Boston, and Seattle to Miami, but the world music audience remains largely unaware of their existence.

In part, this is because norteño music is based on accordion polkas and waltzes. Those who love it may point to the driving rhythms and soulful country vocals as having a classic roots flavor, but to casual outsiders it tends to provoke memories of Polish wedding bands. Meanwhile, the sort of organizations that usually promote immigrant culture are wary because of the Tigres' lyrics. Though they have been more circumspect in recent years, the band built much of its reputation with *corridos* (heroic ballads) about the drug traffickers working on the border between Mexico and the United States.

"I began recording at the apogee of the drug business," explains the group's leader, Jorge Hernández.[*] "And since I'm from Sinaloa [the West Coast state famed as a center of the Mexican drug trade], when I sang in the cantinas they asked me for stories. Still today, if you go to Sinaloa and watch a guy who hires a band or a norteño group, he just wants to hear stories—a love song here and there, but mostly stories. I know, because I was a *cantinero* for many years, I worked in

---

[*] This interview was conducted in Spanish.

Jorge Hernández of Los Tigres del Norte. Photograph © Jack Vartoogian/FrontRowPhotos.

Contents

Tables

Acknowledgements

The editors, contributors and the publisher would like to thank the following for giving kind permission to reproduce material: The *New Scientist* for 'Pioneer's name written in synthetic DNA'; *The Independent* for 'Playing God: The man who would create artificial life'; The Institution of Engineering and Technology for the article in *Flipside* entitled 'Alien Comet Invades Solar System'.

Contributors

Alison Boyle is Curator of Astronomy & Modern Physics at the Science Museum, London, UK where she interprets the collections via gallery, web and other outputs. She is also a science writer.

Mark Brake is an author, broadcaster and communicator of science. He is Professor of Science Communication at the University of Glamorgan, UK. He is recognized as a leading academic in the field and has published many books, including *Different Engines: How Science Drives Fiction and Fiction Drives Science* and *FutureWorld*, with his colleague Neil Hook.

Karen Bultitude is Senior Lecturer in Science Communication at the University of the West of England, UK. Her expertise lies in direct (face-to-face) methods of communicating scientific messages and in 2008 she was awarded the prestigious Joshua Phillips Memorial Prize for Science Engagement.

Neil Hook is Lecturer in Science Communication at the University of Glamorgan, UK which he combines with his work as an Anglican priest.

Toby Murcott is science writer, journalist, broadcaster and producer. He lectures in Science Communication at the University of Glamorgan, UK.

Emma Weitkamp is Senior Lecturer in Science Communication, University of the West of England, UK. With wide ranging experience of science writing, she has worked as a medical writer and environmental news editor as well as in public relations. She is also the creator of 'ScienceComics' (http://www.sciencecomics.uwe.ac.uk).

Clare Wilkinson is Senior Lecturer in Science Communication at the University of the West of England, UK. Clare is a sociologist, who has published in a range of journals including *Science Communication* and *Public Understanding of Science*. Clare has recently co-written the book *Nanotechnology, Risk and Communication* for Palgrave Macmillan.

Introduction

Mark Brake and Emma Weitkamp

In 1929, the legendary British theoretical physicist Paul Dirac hit Wisconsin. 'The purest soul in physics', as he was described by Niels Bohr, Dirac was in the north central United States to deliver a series of lectures at a local university.

Dirac was an unsung genius of physics, and had made a stunning break-through in 1928. Combining the theories of quantum mechanics and Einstein's special relativity, Dirac had predicted the existence of antimatter, which makes up, at least in principle, half the universe.

Local reporters gathered to interview the great man. Though they lived during an era in which the cult of personality was far less pronounced than it is today, they'd all heard of Einstein. Besides, competition in journalism was keener than ever. Broadcast radio was in its infancy. Only earlier that decade, radio emerged as a novel means of communication, a fitting medium to report the new and exhilarating science of quantum mechanics.

Had the local reporters done their research, they may have found cause for concern. Dirac was achingly shy. Later, he even wanted to refuse the Nobel Prize in order to shun the publicity. But the scoop of journalists gathered around the esteemed professor knew little of his reticence.

Finally, a reporter from the *Wisconsin State Journal* broke the silence,

'Now doctor will you give me in a few words the low-down on all your investigations?'

We can imagine the scene: the question posed, the reporters waiting, with baited-breath in anticipation of the professor's profound reply.

'No', replied Dirac.

The story of Paul Dirac's near-silent skirmish with the press is an amusing one, especially so in today's world of the more media-savvy scientist.

Communicating science to the public – whether through the media, museums, or outreach – is now a burgeoning global industry, a rapidly growing field of multidisciplinary practice, education and research, throughout the world.

For in the last two or three decades, it seems as though scientists have been issued with an edict: *communicate, or else!* Gone are the days when indulging in the popular communication of science seemed like professional suicide. Nowadays, each and every aspiring young researcher is also expected to be a

1

practitioner, someone who is prepared to take science out of the laboratory, and into the culture.

Stemming from an initial concern amongst scientists and politicians that the wider public lacked an understanding and appreciation of science, the field has grown and developed rapidly. Grounded originally in a philosophy that saw the 'public' as lacking an understanding and appreciation of science, the field has now moved away from didactic, top-down approaches to communication to consider more inclusive approaches to communication that emphasize the need to engage a wider range of so-called 'publics' in decisions about science (see for example, Miller 2001).

In fact, Public Engagement in Science and Technology (PEST) continues to be a key priority as governments around the globe seek to encourage citizens to participate in debates about new and emerging science, such as nanotechnology and stem cells. Tackling global problems, such as climate change, whether on a personal or societal level also requires citizens to engage with science and technology. As stated in the House of Lords report, Science and Society,

> direct dialogue with the public should move from being an optional add-on to science based policy making and to the activities of research organisations and learned institutions, and should become a normal and integral part of the process. (House of Lords 2000)

This priority to engage the public with science and technology underpins the theories and strategies that are explored in the following chapters, which discuss both practical techniques and the historical developments which underpin the philosophy of science communication and public engagement. Science communication focuses on dialogue between scientists, policy makers and laypeople. The one-way deficit philosophy of science communication, which was predicated on the idea that the lay person was somehow deficient in his knowledge of science, is now largely out of fashion.

This doesn't mean that all science communication activities need to involve dialogue. Strategies that inform the public of new scientific research or excite the public about scientific discoveries are still important. The point is that the public are seen has having a role to play in decisions about science, such as funding and regulation.

> The implementation of [Public Engagement with Science] in the science policy arena has helped to develop and articulate new understanding of and expectations for the relationship between science and publics in policy making and other contexts. (The Centre for Advancement of Informal Science Education – CAISE 2009)

New developments, new media

In exploring the opportunities and challenges faced by science communicators, this book delves into such wide ranging approaches to science communication as fiction, film and festivals. Using such cultural forms may offer opportunities to reach out to new audiences or those who have traditionally been hard to reach. Music festivals, such as Glastonbury, may offer novel ways to reach young people, often one of the hardest groups to engage.

Other cultural institutions, such as museums, print and broadcast media have their own strengths and weaknesses. Museums and hands-on science centres, for example, reach family audiences and school groups offering the potential for in-depth engagement. However, these venues do not reach all socioeconomic groups equally and the depth of engagement varies depending on the event and activity. Broadcast and print media are traditionally seen as fairly passive ways of informing or educating people, but may reach large audiences.

New opportunities to reach out to and engage a wide range of people with science are developing at a rapid pace. The potential of social networking sites, podcasts and blogs for science communication remains under-researched. These new media may offer exciting and interactive ways of reaching both new and traditional audiences. The 'anytime, anywhere' nature of these media may appeal to the 24/7 society we now live in. Certainly they provide varied and as yet under-explored opportunities for creative approaches to PEST.

In sum, the tools, techniques and strategies available to science communicators continue to grow. As scientific issues clash with societal concerns the need for PEST will surely grow. Global social issues such as sustainability, distribution of natural resources and healthcare require citizen involvement in science policy both on local, national and international levels. These indicators point to a continuing need for the public to engage with science and technology.

This book about the communication of science is designed to help science communicators work through all of these demands. It provides an introduction to the main methods and issues of the field, in simple, clear and direct language. It is structured, presented and packaged in such a way as to provide an attractive and affordable introductory pocket guide to science communication, providing a must-have basic text for anyone involved in the field.

This book includes practical advice and exercises, grounded in those aspects of communication and learning theory likely to be of most immediate and practical use to teachers, trainers and students alike. The presented material is also accompanied by a sufficient historical and social context to make for an easier and more informative read.

The text also provides the student of science communication with a brief history of the field, together with practical advice on communicating science. Areas of science communication covered in subsequent chapters, fall into several broad areas: science communication between scientists, between scientists and the public, and between scientists and policy makers; communication on science and technology issues carried out within and between governments, businesses and other organizations, and between governments, businesses, etc. and the general public and the role of the traditional and new media in science communication. The emphasis of the book is on providing practical guidance, a so-called 'how to' approach, but within the context of the main theoretical movements both underpinning the field and driving it forward today.

Structure of the book

Introducing Science Communication is presented in two distinct sections. Part I, Science Communication: In Context, comprises those chapters that are more theoretically informed and provide the background material to the practical guide presented in Part II, Science Communication: In Practice.

Part I opens with The History and Development of Science and its Communication, the subject of Chapter 1, which focuses on the nature of science and the place of science within society. Given that this book is a guide to science communication, it would not be complete without an in-depth introduction to the nature of science itself. The field has often neglected such an articulation of science. And yet an understanding of the nature of science cannot be taken for granted. Especially as fields such as history, philosophy and sociology reveal the challenges in the public's engagement with science and also that controversies in the scientific sphere are often a reflection of deeper political struggles in society itself. This chapter, therefore, provides a context and rationale for the communication of science by locating science firmly in a historical and social context. It highlights the role of science in economic development, as well as in social progress. The chapter considers the history of the practical nature of science and its relationship to technique, in order to develop an appreciation of some of the major ways in which these relations inform the communication of science.

The link between science and culture is explored in Chapter 2. Science in Popular Culture considers how science informs and contributes to popular cultural forms, including literature, cinema and theatre. The chapter focuses specifically on science in fictional contexts, considering how science is used and portrayed in these media and the potential of various cultural forms to contribute to the science communication agenda. The role of science advisors to cinema and theatre is considered and the role of scientists as 'mass media' personalities is also scrutinized.

The final chapter of Part I is on the subject of Science and the Citizen, presented in Chapter 3. This chapter discusses recent movements in science communication. A range of ideas is considered, from the now largely outdated 'Scientific Literacy' approach, to the more inclusive public engagement approach. The chapter considers the role of science communication in formal education from the policy drivers in the United States and Europe, which emphasize the need to encourage more young people into scientific careers, through to the role of learning theory and science education in the field of science communication. The importance of interactions between science and society is also considered in relation to its impact on science communication, along with strategies for developing science communication initiatives based on dialogue, such as Citizens' Juries.

The practical aspects of science communication are presented in Part II. Chapter 4, Writing Science, provides an introduction to science journalism, considering the needs of both readers and editors. The chapter outlines the key principles of good writing and gives practical advice on finding interesting science stories, whilst exploring the tools and techniques needed to write for a variety of print and online media outlets.

A brief history of broadcast media from radio to early TV is provided in Chapter 5, Broadcasting Science. Readers are introduced to the world of broadcast media, exploring the roles and professions involved in creating both radio and TV programmes. Radio and TV genre are placed in the context of presenting ideas to potential producers and programme makers, either for entire programmes or simply to convey a specific scientific development. The chapter provides guidance for the aspiring broadcast science communicator, including interview techniques and an exploration of the up and coming related media, such as podcasting and videocasting (e.g., YouTube), which may be more readily accessed by aspiring producers.

Practical demonstrations of scientific developments and ideas have a long history and provide an exciting opportunity to communicate science. Chapter 6, Presenting Science, explores the principles and pitfalls of presenting science in public. A facet of successful science communication, whether through a live demonstration or broadcast documentary, is a thorough understanding of the audience. In this chapter, readers will explore the nature of different audiences and how to cater for them. Practical advice on planning, preparing, presenting and evaluating 'SciComm' events, such as talks, lectures and so on, is provided, as well as tips on organizing events along with the dos and don'ts of live experiments and demonstrations.

Science museums from the early Ashmolean in Oxford to the present day have played a key role in communicating science. Chapter 7, Communicating Science in Museums and Science Centres, considers styles and trends in public exhibitions of science and the origins and rise of the hands-on science centre and exploratorium. The pros and cons of artefact-based communication are considered, as is museum visitor behaviour, along with practical advice on creating and evaluating traditional and hands-on science exhibits.

References and further reading

CAISE (2009), Many Experts, Many Audiences: Public Engagement with Science and Informal Science Education, A CAISE Inquiry Group Report. Available online at: http://caise.insci.org/resources

House of Lords (2000), Science and Society, Session 1999–2000, Third Report, HL paper 38, February.

Miller, S. (2001), Public Understanding of Science at the Crossroads, *Public Understanding of Science* 10, 115–120.

Research Council UK – RCUK/DIUS (2008), *Public Attitudes to Science 2008: A Survey*. London: People, Science and Policy Limited. Available online at: http://www.rcuk.ac.uk/sis/pas.htm

Part I

Science Communication:
In Context

The History and Development of Science and Its Communication

Mark Brake

1

In such a practical guide to communicating science, considerable care should be taken to introduce what science is, expose its practical nature and its relationship to technique, its relationship to society, politics and culture. In this way, we can better understand the context of the practical topics to be covered in the chapters that follow. That is the job of this introductory chapter.

The box below outlines the main general and theoretical points covered by this chapter are.

LEARNING POINTS

- What is science?
- The practical nature of science and its relationship to technique;
- The relationship of science to society, politics and culture;
- The history and development of science and its communication.

What is science?

This chapter aims to give an account of the history and development of science and its communication. In so doing, it will touch upon the relations between the evolution of science and that of other features of human history and culture. Our ultimate purpose is to develop an appreciation of some of the major ways in which these relations inform the communication of science.

Society today, in its material features, would be impossible without science. Indeed, many contemporary intellectual and moral aspects of civilization are also deeply influenced by science. The dissemination of scientific ideas has been the most crucial dynamic in the shaping of contemporary thought. But society is also faced with great fears. Fears of annihilation through weapons of mass destruction and concerns over climate change and a mushrooming global population sit alongside the hope of longer and better lives through the application of medical science.

Progress in science seems to bring pitfalls, as well as promise. The way science manifests itself in society, its freedoms and secrecies, its use in education as well as in war, its relationship to governments and culture, all this presents the communicator of science with a host of great challenges. How are such questions to be addressed, if at all?

Some object that most science is uncontroversial, the great majority of its research findings rather innocuous and unremarkable. In their book, *The Golem: What You Should Know About Science*, sociologists of science Harry Collins and Trevor Pinch argue that only controversial science need be known to the layperson, even though 'most science is uncontroversial' (Collins and Pinch 1998).

Thankfully, a growing consensus is at hand. Ultimately, for the sake of survival, problems such as climate change must be addressed; the communicator of science engaging with the public must confront the controversial. And communication will mean little if it is not guided by the deeper lessons to be learned from a critical study of history.

A working critical understanding of the relationship between science and society is essential, which requires knowledge of the history of science and of society. In science, more than in any other human endeavour, it is vital to look to the past in order to understand the now, and to plan the future.

For too long there has been a rather unadventurous idea about the nature of scientific knowledge. This idea firmly held that current knowledge is the best available wisdom on science, that it has somehow replaced and supplanted all preceding scientific knowledge. In its turn, current knowledge too will become obsolete, displaced by future facts. All useful previous knowledge is subsumed by that of the present; the mistakes of the ignorant, consigned to the dustbin of history.

Take the example of *The Times* of London. In reporting the alleged 'victory' of Einsteinian physics over its Newtonian counterpart in November 1919, the editors were moved to declare,

> it is confidently believed by the greatest experts that enough has been done to overthrow the certainty of ages and to require a new philosophy of the universe, a philosophy that will sweep away nearly all that has hitherto been accepted as the axiomatic basis of physical thought. (Gregory and Miller 1998)

Einstein himself was greatly embarrassed. When, on 28 November 1919, he was invited to write his own article on relativity for *The Times*, he was at pains to point out that,

> No one must think that Newton's great creation can be overthrown in any real sense by this or any other theory. His clear and wide ideas will forever retain their significance as the foundations on which our modern conceptions of physics have been built. (Gregory and Miller 1998).

Thankfully, many scientists are starting to see the appalling cost of continuing an ignorance of history; for with it, any intelligent understanding of the place of science in society is lost. Armed with knowledge of the past, the communicator of science can better communicate the grand ongoing drama of the use and abuse of science.

It's not so long ago that both scientists and the public firmly believed that science and technology led straight to nothing but progress. At first, such a suggestion was dangerous speculation; heresy, even. But, by the time of the Renaissance, as early as 1619, German theologian Johan Valentin Andreae was to declare, 'It is inglorious to despair of Progress' (Ginsberg 1953).

And so the idea of progress was born. It was not until the nineteenth century, however, with the immense potential for change through science and industry, that the notion of progress became a self-evident truth. It is hardly the case now. Not when the latent power of science can lay waste to the planet.

The communicator of science needs to understand science. Not just the technical detail, but how science is the catalyst by which our societies are being swiftly changed. And to understand how, we need not look only to the present. We must look also to the past, at how science evolved, how science has responded to the successive forms of society, and how it has helped shape them.

Of course, scientists don't run society. They are not ultimately responsible for the troubles of our times. They don't have some kind of operational power over civilization. But the use of science is not totally out of their hands.

Consider the case of the Manhattan Project, the allied scientific research program to develop the first nuclear weapon of mass destruction, during the Second World War. English physicist Freeman Dyson has clearly suggested that in fact, 'scientists rather than generals took the initiative in getting nuclear weapons programs started' (Dyson 1984), and that they were, 'motivated to build weapons by feelings of professional pride as well as of patriotic duty' (Dyson 1984) rather than strategic needs.

So scientists must face up to the new century. The days when they traditionally attempted to evade responsibility in the name of the disinterested search for truth are long gone. They disappeared when the Cold War began. In a twenty-first century of global warming, want and warfare, a lack of social responsibility looks increasingly bankrupt.

The Manhattan Project's lead scientist, Robert Oppenheimer, spoke for many physicists when he said, 'In some sort of crude sense which no vulgarity, no humour, no overstatement can quite extinguish, the physicists have known sin; and this is a knowledge which they cannot lose' (Dowling 1986). Oppenheimer believed that if atomic bombs were to be added as new weapons to the arsenals of a warring world, 'then the time will come when mankind will curse the names of Los Alamos and Hiroshima. The people of this world must unite or they will perish' (Dowling 1986).

The scope of science

What is the significance and scope of science? It may seem reasonable to begin with a definition of science, but its true nature is not that straightforward.

For science is ancient. It may not always have been known by that name, but what we understand today as science has developed over thousands of years. It has passed through so many cultures and societies, evolved through many metamorphoses; any attempted definition would effectively deny its evolving nature. Einstein had the same idea when he said,

> Science as something existing and complete is the most objective thing known to man. But science in the making, science as an end to be pursued, is as subjective and psycho-logically conditioned as any other branch of human endeavour – so much so, that the question 'what is the purpose and meaning of science?' receives quite different answers at different times and from different sorts of people. (Einstein 1935)

In short, the notion of a definition is unhelpful. For science is a human activity, an inseparable feature of the process of social evolution. It evolves and changes, is always in a state of flux. As the pre-Socratic Greek philoso-pher Heraclitus was perhaps the first to point out, everything flows, science included.

Science is variable, and given the increasing pace of change during the twentieth century, the changeability of science is its only constant. Neither has it always been separated out from the rest of human activity and culture. In ancient times, it was merely one aspect of the work of the sophist. During the late Middle Ages, it would have been an elemental feature of the job of the alchemist, or the astrologer.

Only since the scientific revolution, and more specifically the seventeenth century, has science been considered autonomous, independent from other human activity. In fact, its autonomy may only be a passing phase. In future, science may come to infuse all social life, once more having no discrete existence.

Key features of science

The field of science communication is broad. It embraces the perspectives of many practitioners: scientists, historians, sociologists, journalists, communi-cation theorists, politicians and philosophers. Its chief area of discourse is the public's engagement with science; its main aim is to somehow improve this engagement.

Given that this book is a guide to science communication, it would not be complete without an in-depth introduction to the nature of science itself. The field has often neglected such an articulation of science. And yet an understanding of the nature of science cannot be taken for granted, especially as fields such as history, philosophy and sociology reveal challenges in the public's engagement with science and also that controversies in the scientific sphere are a reflection of deeper political struggles in society itself.

With this in mind, this chapter looks at the chief characteristics of science. We can identify at least five features: science as an institution; science as a method; science as a body of knowledge; science as the key driver of the economy; and science as a worldview.

Not all of these features have always been present, of course. Science can only be considered an institution, and as a key driver of the economy, since the industrial revolution. But the influence of the scientific method, and its power as a worldview, can be traced back to early forms that held some considerable sway in antiquity.

Furthermore, the idea of science as a body of knowledge, as a cumulative tradition, is the very basis of science. This tradition, which links science strongly to technique, was the knowledge passed from craftsman to apprentice, elder to novice, existing from the earliest of societies and cultures. Indeed, it began long before science developed as a method, discrete from everyday practice and folklore.

Institutional science

Science today is part of the establishment, an institution in which thousands of professional scientists are employed, often after a protracted period of training. And yet, even the word 'scientist' itself is a recent invention, being coined only in 1840 by English polymath William Whewell.

Perhaps the first embryonic institution of science was Plato's Academy in classical Athens. Set up in approximately 385 BC, it was the first institution of higher learning in the western world. Here, for almost half a century, Plato himself taught at the Academy, named after the hero Academus. Plato defined the character of the institution, directed the tone of its communications.

Above the gate, he had written the legend 'Let No One Ignorant of Mathematics Enter Here'. Not exactly an invitation to all-comers. The goal of the Academy was to discuss and communicate pure knowledge, mainly astronomy, mathematics and music. But it was abstract learning, one suspicious of experiment. It was an activity restricted to the reading of texts; not wisdom derived from a close study of nature, with all its twists, turns and trickery.

Within these walls, Plato produced an immense body of communicated work. He became the first philosopher of antiquity whose writings survived, not in pieces of parchment, but in sheer bulk. The extent of Plato's work is vast. Its scope covers a great part of the ancient sphere of knowledge; his dialogues alone comprise a volume the length of the Bible. And here lies the answer to Plato's enormous influence. His legacy was a vast body of communicated knowledge.

The Academy is the distant ancestor of all today's universities, seats of learning and societies of science. The institution did not stop with Plato's death. Until it was closed in 529 AD, for almost one thousand years the Athenian Academy continued, poring over the works of Plato, seeking knowledge of truth and beauty for its own sake.

The ancient Greek philosophers were gentlemen of leisure. Indeed, during most of history, science has been an amateur occupation of gentlemen. Only those in positions of wealth and power had the time and money to afford the hobby of discovery and experiment. The noted Welsh philosopher John Dee, for example, was consultant to Queen Elizabeth I and sometimes known as 'The Queen's Conjuror'; her professional court astrologer as well as her court physician. Science in those days of yore was the preserve of the middle or upper classes.

As time passed, the institution of science has become increasingly influential in giving science direction. Indeed, the direction and results of science have always been driven by society, though often not in an exacting way, perhaps the most famous example being the early days of shipbuilding and navigation, when the quest to derive longitude on the open sea became a lucrative aim for both astronomy and empire.

Science has always been driven, and never practised purely for its own good. British biologist Lewis Wolpert has suggested (Wolpert 2002) that scientific knowledge has no moral or ethical value. What's more, 'Science tells us how the world is', apparently, and scientists 'do not appropriate decision-making for themselves'. Wolpert's opinion is flatly contradicted by the facts. We have already witnessed Freeman Dyson's first-hand experience and observations of the Manhattan Project.

Furthermore, in the biography of Fritz Haber, *Between Genius and Genocide: The Tragedy of Fritz Haber, Father of Chemical Warfare*, Dan Charles (Charles 2005) describes how Haber, like many career scientists, lived the life of the German High Command during the First World War. Charles explains that it was Haber who suggested that the military could use clouds of chlorine gas to asphyxiate soldiers in enemy trenches. It didn't take a Nobel laureate to think of using poison gas as a weapon. The idea had been in the air, so to speak, for many years. But it took the audacity and energy of a single deadly chemist, such as Haber, to turn the idea into noxious reality.

By the end of the war, his deadly weapon had killed or injured about 650,000 people on the Western Front. Haber won the Nobel Prize in 1918, for his work in the synthesis of ammonia, important for explosives. Unable to live with a man who worked to such priorities, Clara Haber found her husband's army-issued pistol, and shot herself.

Understandably, many feel that to use science in the pay of profit or warfare is deviant. Others believe that such misuses of science are perhaps a necessary perversion. Nonetheless, science is done for a purpose, and understanding this is important to a more thoughtful approach to the communication of science itself.

The scientific method

Scientific methods have continued to evolve throughout history. They are part of an organic process, which is closely linked to the evolving social character of science. Throughout its history, science has been made up of a combination of procedures, involving the work of the mind and the work of the hand. However, for the greater part of history, mental and manual labour has not always been practised in close cooperation.

Take the example of the telescope:

BOX 1.1   THE TELESCOPE AS AN EXAMPLE

The history of optics is a fascinating episode of the social relationship between theory and technique. The technology that made up the telescope had been known for some time. Ancient civilizations had noticed the curious lens effect produced by, say, transparent crystals, glass spheres full of water or jewels. Indeed, the magnifying effects were something of a fascination.

But it's as though those observations came too soon. In the theories and texts of many ancient Greek and particularly medieval Arab scholars, it is clear that some theory of optics was in existence. The technology to magnify had also been available. And clearly the demand for the technology of magnification in commerce and warfare was legion. But theory was never married to practice, never tallied up to the optical devices that may have been available.

This curious state of affairs can be explained in two related ways: firstly, a social explanation. It's very unusual in history, as we have seen, for scholars and craftsmen to work together, given their difference in social class. This was the case until the European Renaissance, one of the distinguishing features of which was the intensity and distribution of the collaboration between the work of the mind and the work of the hand.

Secondly, the old adage 'a little knowledge is a dangerous thing' may also apply here. Ancient or medieval observations made through transparent crystals, glass spheres or jewels, don't just show things bigger or better. They can also warp and deceive. To the more superstitious mind, a mind not married to rational theory, such optical illusions can make one wary. Sight is the most paradoxical of senses. It is at once the most reliable, and yet the most deluding. Without theory, perhaps you can't really trust what you see.

Perhaps due in part to such vagaries, the study of the methods of science has progressed far more slowly than the study and development of science itself. For the main part, scientists discover things, and only later, and rather ineptly, reflect on the way in which their discovery was made. Nonetheless, different methods have been found useful, in formulating questions, and in finding, testing and using the answers to such questions.

At first, a working scientist would scope the task at hand. Then something is tried out, to see if it will work. The outcomes of this attempt are observed and noted. To put it less colloquially, the method can be loosely described as experiment and observation. It is, of course, crucial to know how and what to observe. Scientists generally observe in order to discover results and relations, which are, as much as they can be, independent of their own opinions.

That's not to say scientists have no wilful intent. Once more, a study of history will reveal the reality. A conscious, deliberate and practical plan is near essential for discovery. But there has to be a careful balance of the human and non-human elements: as much as they possibly can, working scientists must be immune to emotive responses, in order to attain their objective in the non-human world.

Gregory and Miller (1998) report the views of chemistry professor Henry Bauer on the question of the scientific method. Bauer considers the notion an obstacle to achieving good science communication due to the fallacy that 'there exists an entity called "science" about which sweeping generalisations can validly be made' (Bauer 1994).

Bauer's view is that the practice of science is a series of ill-defined puzzle-solving exercises, which then go through a 'reality therapy' check, before being accepted as 'true'. His conclusion is nonetheless positive, suggesting that we cannot only take collective pride in the science we know, but also in the fact that we know how to go about learning more.

The results and relations discovered by scientific experiment constitute a body of knowledge. The logical part of science seeks to use names, symbols and formulae in order to derive a sufficiently consistent set of hypotheses and theories.

These relations are dressed up in the languages of science, languages that have evolved to provide the most exacting descriptions possible. The languages are not inherently alien, but may have an alienating affect upon those who are not familiar with their common usage in the field. Since scientific language is far too useful to ditch, it is the job of the science communicator to translate it into everyday explanations that are more easily understood, at least until the ideas of science become as proverbial in everyday life as its technological devices.

Stratagems of science

As to the stratagems of science, there is no absolute need for a deliberate and conscious approach to planning science. In the past, there certainly was no conscious direction or policy to seek advance. But, neither has progress in science been accidental. For the majority of time, some scheme, part conscious, part unconscious, seems to have been in operation. Progress has taken place, in the main, through economic need, scientific ideas taking a back seat as a driver of initiative.

Witness some telling examples.

The seventeenth-century challenge of finding longitude at sea effectively led to the derivation of Newton's laws. The crisis in sericulture in France in the nineteenth century led to Pasteur's theory of disease. And the race to the atom bomb greatly developed the knowledge of atomic physics. As late as 1942, many scientists still thought the bomb impossible, but the forefront of nuclear research was pushed forward, more than any other scientific endeavour in history, corrupted by the fear of rivals and supercharged by vast material resources.

For some, a lack of conscious planning has been a major problem for science. For long periods of time, the labour of scientists has focused on solving a small number of single issues, refining the solutions. This tendency of science to work within narrow limits, constrains any other tendency it may have to seek challenges outside of this rather narrow framework.

Only the exceptional scientists, such as Kepler, Newton and Faraday, have set their own agenda and sought challenges of their own design. Kepler and Newton each set themselves the task of knowing the mind of God, a rather daunting duty. Faraday, on the other hand, focused his sights on the challenge of discovering the links between the discrete forces of nature: light, heat, electricity and magnetism.

Today's planning of science is collective, rather than individual: big science, rather than little. The lucrative reward of science to modern society is so great that no country is able to compete unless it makes a planned use of its scientists. This progression of the increasing use of science in society is one of the reasons that the communication of science is valued so highly. It's likely to become increasingly so in the future.

Finally, how is science different to other intellectual aspects, such as the humanities, art or religion? Arguably, and the point has been argued many times, of course, the main points of divergence of science from other disciplines centre on its practical application. Science is a discipline concerned with how things are done.

When we think of science in this practical way, we can identify its functions and how they relate to technique. So, as a body of cumulative knowledge, science is about action, as well as fact. Its origin and development lie in its concern with techniques to provide for human needs. Indeed, it helps greatly to think of science as a recipe, it tells you how to carry out certain tasks, should you need to do them.

From this practical perspective, then, science is not merely a matter of thought. It is thought constantly translated into practice, constantly refined by technique. The history of science shows new aspects of science continually developing in this way.

Science as a body of knowledge

Another important aspect of science, and one of which every dutiful science communicator should be aware, is the evolutionary development of science as a cumulative body of knowledge. It is arguable as to whether science is truly unique in having a vast reserve of historical observations and experience on which practitioners may draw.

Of course, little of this collective compendium of historical information is unerring in its accuracy or relevance, to a working contemporary scientist. But it is adequate enough for the practitioner to carry on where such work left off, and not have to start afresh. Perhaps a suitable parallel is that of the practitioner in law, since law too is in some ways an evidentiary and cumulative system of knowledge.

From this perspective, science can be seen as progressive, a growing discipline, made up of successions of thoughts and deliberations, observations and activities of a host of previous practitioners. In this aspect, science can be considered as the net outcome of all its endeavours up to that date. Unlike religion, perhaps, it is not a discipline preserved in amber, a field whose primary function is to conserve an ancient 'truth'. No, science is changing, cumulative, constantly under repair, but always in use.

It is well for the communicator of science to remember that practitioners in their field are in many senses consciously motivated to change the consensus, alter the established truth, rather than preserve it – at least in principle.

Like other human endeavours, science is a living body of knowledge. But whereas great works of literature and art live on through arbitrary interpretation, the works of science can be verified by direct and repeatable experiments in the material world. Whether present or past, each advance in science can be exposed to experiment and examination. The success of science lies in its ability to apply its schema to inanimate material systems, in the case of physics, or living organisms in the case of biology.

It is interesting and instructive to look at the way in which this living body of knowledge has evolved, to examine the pattern of scientific advance. History shows a distinct sequence of the emergence of the different disciplines of science. Generally speaking, the order is: mathematics, astronomy, mechanics, physics, chemistry and biology.

This developmental time sequence of the sciences is fascinating. It appears to fit very well to the patterns of social advance. Notice how the sequence corresponds quite closely to the practical uses that were expected, if not demanded, of science by ruling classes at different times.

In ancient times, science derived from the techniques that arose from humanity's concern with the natural environment. For example, from the beginning of recorded history and the development of surplus, mathematics arose out of the need to make calculations relating to taxation and commerce, or to measure land. Observations of the sky were used to determine the seasons, an important factor in knowing when to plant crops, as well as in understanding the length of the year. These priestly functions gave rise to astronomy, of course.

Only much later did interest arise in the control of inanimate forces. The demands of the new textile industry, the interest of the emerging manufacturers of the eighteenth century, gave rise to contemporary chemistry. The more complex sciences, such as medicine and biology, were developed through the study of the subject itself, with practically no input from the simpler sciences, such as mechanics.

When we consider a more detailed example of such a sequence of discovery, other general trends tend to occur. In any specific discipline, a series of associated findings can be identified. The chain of events usually begins with an unexpected and revolutionary discovery, the coming together of fields previously thought unrelated, and ending up with an entirely new field of science.

Consider the case of the Newtonian 'System of the World' associated with the development of the theory of universal gravitation in the late seventeenth century. This long chain of events began at least a century before with Copernicus's revolutionary proposal of the sun-centred planetary system, which led to the coming together of Galileo's experiments in terrestrial dynamics with Kepler's celestial mechanics, and ended up with Newton's synthesis of the new mechanical worldview of the universe – a worldview which was to dominate physics until the early twentieth century.

This brief portrait above, in which three hundred years of physics is reduced to the distilled essence of the work of just four men, highlights a problem. Communicators of science should be sceptical of the conventional view of the advancement of science. This view presents the evolution of science as that of a peaceful, smooth and uninterrupted development. It is both one-sided and false.

The view fails to consider two essential elements of the progress of science. The first is long periods of investigations, which rely upon a gradual advance of tradition and custom. This first element is the fruit of many ordinary thinkers and workers. The second element is the revolutionary tipping points. In spite of all gradualness, an innovatory leap leads to decisive change. This element is usually associated with the 'great men of science'.

The 'great men' myth has led to a false idea of science, one which suggests that progress in science is due solely to the genius of great men, irrespective of factors such as culture, society and economy. We're expected to believe that these masterminds just dream this stuff up out of thin air. Many conservative histories of science are rooted in the 'great men' myth. They are little more than a series of naïve narratives of great discoverers, each with their own momentous and revelatory insight into the secrets of nature.

Let's be clear: great men, and women, have been a crucial factor in the development of science. But their contribution should be studied and communicated in context, and not in isolation from their contemporary social setting. An inability to see this often leads to the use of redundant words like 'brainwave' or 'genius' to explain away those eureka moments of discovery.

In truth, conventional narratives devalue great 'men'. Such accounts of their work are too narrow and too idle to realize that great people are products of their time. Only by recognizing that they are subject to the same sway of social influence, the same sorry compulsions, is their plight realized and their stature enhanced. Indeed, the greater the person, the more they are immersed in the milieu of their days. They become more important. For only by seizing the moment chanced by their times are they able to make that innovatory leap that leads to critical change.

Nor is the 'great men' myth specific to science. It applies to thinkers in any cultural field. But the hold of the myth on histories of science retained its grip far longer than on histories of culture and society. No effective discovery can be made in any field without the necessary groundwork of thousands of relatively minor workers. It is on the basis of this painstaking work that great 'men' make crucial discoveries.

Societies produce populations with a vast array of mental abilities. Relatively few seek a career in science, though more have the opportunity of doing so in the twenty-first century than ever before. Scientists are likely to differ greatly in their characteristics. But this much they will have in common: they are creatures of the culture in which they swim. Differing individual mental faculty gives a great variety to science. But imposed social and cultural controls and influences give science its unity, and make possible the collective effort of science to understand and master our environment.

Science as a key driver of the economy

What is the communicator of science to make of the relationship between science and industry? What is its relationship to business and commerce, and how have these links evolved throughout history?

Arguably, these questions frame one of the most important aspects of science, and one that has led to its pivotal position in twenty-first century civilization: the part that science has played, and continues to play, in the creation of wealth, goods, food and comfort – in short, science's role as a key driver of the economy.

Once again to establish a deeper understanding, a historical perspective is needed. This shows that science arose as a specific type of social pursuit, a means of gaining control over nature. This dominion over the environment was achieved in phases, each distinguished by the emergence of another material technique. This is why we still talk in material terms, when speaking of our archaeological past. The prehistory of the Stone Age, the metalworking techniques that allowed tools to become more common in the Bronze Age, the societal changes in agriculture, religion and culture associated with the Iron Age, and the mass production associated with the Machine Age. For the last half-century, we've been living in the Space Age, though the prospect of the fleet and nimble starships of fiction is fast receding.

To be of use, materials must be teased and shaped, fashioned into some form that can be used. Indeed, even something as basic as an axe must be hewn from ground stone. And this process of taking and teasing materials into tools to fulfil the needs of primitive man also marks the start of science itself. The techniques associated with tool-making, or the procedures used to accomplish a specific activity or task, are an early form of science. If you consider a technique as a method of doing a task, then science is a method of knowing how to do it, so that it can be done better. The origin of science lies in this activity, and its growth developed out of intimate association with the means of production.

We spoke earlier of progress in science, long periods of investigations and revolutionary tipping points. History shows that research in technique leads to reform, and research in pure science leads to revolution. So it shouldn't be surprising to find that science has a bumpy past: revolutionary leaps in progress, then long phases of gradual advance.

When another tipping point occurs, it may often happen in another country. We have discussed the idea that progress in science is not accidental, and that progress takes place, in the main, through economic need. And this progress has been truly international – from the cradle of civilization in Mesopotamia, to the dawn of rational thought in ancient Greece; from the rekindling of the ancient wisdom by the Islamic Empire of the Middle Ages, to the flowering of Renaissance culture in Western Europe; from the Netherlands and France, to Britain, the engine room of the industrial revolution.

In all that time, science and trade have been bound. At first, science lagged behind trade, but since the days of industry, science has decided the pace of production. To paraphrase a great science communicator, science developed out of the hand axe, it led to the creation of the atom bomb.

Sitting amid the revolutionary explosions of activity are the periods of relative quiescence. Typical of these is the so-called Dark Ages, when in Western Europe at least, trade was at a low level, and the localized nature of feudal system prevented rapid progress. These periods of stasis cannot be put down to science itself. They merely reflect a phase of relative inactivity, when social factors meant that men of learning did not concern themselves with matters of economy.

For most of history, advances in technique, and therefore science, have developed as a result of the direct benefit they provided for particular people or social classes. This would often, naturally, be to the disadvantage of others, sometimes so much so that, as in the case of warfare, it leads to their annihilation. Indeed, war has sometimes been described as the engine of history. It is also an engine of science, a perpetual spring of technical invention. Ultimately, societies depend upon the social relations of production and the associated advantage of one social class over another.

Science too depends on economy. It is the techniques of science that act as a catalyst of production that lead to change. When the economy is in transition, and production is going through rapid change, science is at the forefront. The social class that is in the position of power, not only provides impetus to the change, but also recognizes in science its potential to transform production.

Simply speaking, once in power, this ruling class is keen to eliminate any competition, and so there is less encouragement for innovation in science and technique. For example, when the power rested with the Church in the Dark

Ages, their greatest scholar, St Augustine, was at pains to point out that there was no need to do or communicate science:

> When, then, the question is asked what we are to believe in regard to religion, it is not necessary to probe into the nature of things, as was done by those whom the Greeks call physici; nor need we be in alarm lest the Christian should be ignorant of the force and number of the elements: the motion, and order; and eclipses of the heavenly bodies; the form of the heavens; the species and the natures of animals, plants, stones, fountains, rivers, mountains; about chronology and distances; the signs of coming storms; and a thousand other things which those philosophers either have found out, or think they have found out.... It is enough for the Christian to believe that the only cause of all created things, whether heavenly or earthly, whether visible or invisible, is the goodness of the Creator, the one true God; and that nothing exists but Himself that does not derive its existence from Him. (St Augustine, ed. Marcus Dods 1870)

Looking more deeply than Augustine, we can see the complex relationship of social and material factors, such as the ebb and flow of necessary skills, labour and products, which also make up part of the picture of the rise and fall of both science and economy.

The social nature of science

It's also worth considering the social nature of science. Science is fundamentally a learned vocation. In this respect it contrasts sharply with the practice and technique from which it developed. Unlike technique, which is passed on through custom and tradition, science is communicated and disseminated through journals and books, and previously through scrolls and papyrus.

Due to its very nature of being an abstraction of practice, from the very beginning the job of science has been restricted to a minority of people, those with the ability to engage in this abstraction, and gain recognition for doing so. This situation has had a distinct impact on the social nature of science.

Given that science has been from the very beginning a rather elite profession, its growth has been understandably impeded. There have undoubtedly been a great number of talented people who potentially may have contributed to science. But the majority of people have been kept out of its practice, restricted in their access to books and other cultural artefacts of learning.

As we have mentioned previously with the case study of the telescope, for the greater part of history, mental and manual labour have rarely been practised in close cooperation. The social nature of science as an elite practice has greatly constrained a combination of the work of the mind with the work of the hand. Only with the scientific revolution, and especially after the industrial revolution, did those doing science begin to understand the practical needs of everyday life.

It's little wonder the great mass of people have always been sceptical and suspicious of science. From the first city-states in ancient times, science has been associated with a ruling and oppressing elite. No matter how philanthropic their philosophers may have seemed, most people viewed advance with considerable doubt. Progress more often than not meant enslavement or redundancy.

Ancient scientists were looked upon as shaman. Arthur C. Clarke's observation that any sufficiently advanced technology is indistinguishable from magic springs to mind here. To primitive people, the first scientists must indeed have seemed like magicians capable of boundless mischief. This conviction carried on into the classical world, where common opinion identified the philosophers of the day with the despised oligarchy of the Roman Empire.

In the medieval world, the picture changed little. In contrast to classical times, where science and technique were restricted to the city-states, in feudal times there was a more widespread use of science and technology, particularly throughout the lands of Western Europe. But still the need for useful science was kept to a minimum. This was an age of faiths. And any intellectual effort was instead ploughed into a radical new aspect of civilization: ordered religion.

Even after the scientific and industrial revolutions, the same popular and sceptical response to the now-mechanized progress of science was to be found in the Luddites of the early nineteenth century. H.G. Wells portrayed the same scepticism to mechanized progress in *The War of the Worlds*. In his story, the key to the power of the invading Martians is their technology. Their tripods tower over men physically, their superior machines instruments of human oppression. In the book, Wells evidently has the Martians brutally colonize Earth, but announces that

> before we judge them too harshly we must remember what ruthless and utter destruction our own species has wrought...upon its own inferior races....Are we such apostles of mercy as to complain if the Martians warred in the same spirit? (Wells 1898)

We can better understand Wells's words if we take a non-Eurocentric stance on progress in science, one which looks at the export of science and technology to developing countries. Such an export can be viewed as unsympathetic at best and purely exploitative at worst. The exported technology is often military and destabilizing, or greatly disruptive, such as the replacement of food crops by cash crops. One journalist was moved to suggest that famine-torn Africa was dying 'because in its ill-planned, ill-advised attempt to "modernise" itself, it has cut itself in pieces' (Journalist Lloyd Timberlake, quoted in Gregory and Miller 1998).

It seems that throughout history, the social nature of science, its separation of theory and practice, has been a major obstacle to the free advance of science. Nevertheless, the fact that science was restricted, controlled by those who were literate, numerate, and could debate and communicate in the received way, was of enormous importance to its development at some points in our history.

When we consider the natural world, in its awful and dense complexity, words are often very limited if we are attempting to convey precise conceptual meaning. Folkloric traditions explaining the custom and practice of proven use can only go so far. At some point, practice was abstracted, necessarily so. Specific elements of practice, say the use of moments and levers, would be debated in terms of a theory to refine that practice.

And this step, of developing generalized abstractions out of observed custom, has been crucial to the progress of science itself. For example, the language of communication of the step-by-step refinement of mechanics, by the likes of Galileo and Newton, was not necessarily just a perverse use of an arcane language, used to exclude the uninitiated. They were also a means to an end, a way of generalizing the reach of science into nature, a reach that led to the Scientific Revolution.

All the same, the most revolutionary and vital times of progress were those when the chasm between the classes was closed, at least briefly. At these certain times in history, craftsmen and scholars met on equal terms. It happened during the Scientific Revolution throughout Western Europe; in France, during their great Revolution of the eighteenth century; in the United States, towards the end of the nineteenth century; and, in the early twentieth century.

Consider Renaissance Italy. As is perfectly exemplified by the great engineer, scientist and artist, Leonardo da Vinci, technicians and artists were no longer despised, as they were in the classical world. Art and architecture burgeoned. But so did the practical arts such as pottery, spinning and glass-making.

The craftsman was married to the scholar. The might of the miners and metalworkers was acknowledged, if only because of their key role in the drive to wealth and war. The improved status of such craftsman enabled the renewal of the link between the two for the first time since the early civilizations. And both would benefit from the relationship of knowledge and action.

As Galileo announces at the very beginning of Brecht's greatest play,

> Times are changing, and we now have a new age. In Siena, when I was a young man, I saw some builders, after an argument lasting barely five minutes, discard a centuries old method of moving granite blocks in favour of a new way, a simple rearrangement of the ropes. It was then that I knew that the new age had arrived. What the old books say just isn't good enough anymore. (Brecht 1938)

As the class gap narrowed, many felt a new tongue was needed for science. The style of the English language was drastically simplified in the seventeenth century (Jones 1951, 1953), and the new philosophers were quick to adapt. The first manifestos of science came from the earliest scientific organization, the Royal Society. They vowed to put an end to 'the luxury and redundance of speech' and to

> reject all amplifications, digressions, and swellings of style: to return back to the primitive purity, and shortness, when men deliver'd so many things, almost in an equal number of words ... a close, naked natural way of speaking; positive expressions, clear senses; a native easiness: bringing all things as near the Mathematical plainness, preferring the language of Artizans, Countrymen, and Merchants, before that, of Wits, or Scholars. (Sprat 1667)

In England, there was a feeling that Copernican astronomy had gifted a radical view of the universe as a whole, of science and society as one. The distinction between heavenly and earthly physics had ended. And the radicals aimed at bringing this change down to earth, by ending the distinction between specialists and laymen. They wanted an end to the dominance of Latin, Hebrew and Greek.

The last thing the radicals wanted was for the emerging science to be handed over to a new set of mumbo-jumbo men. Instead, they wanted science, philosophy and politics taught in every parish, by an elected non-specialist. Along with the radical scientists, they wanted science to be rationally applied to the problems of human life.

Indeed, they wanted democratization of all things, a Commonwealth of knowledge in which the yawning gap between the useless specialized scholar and the ill-educated practical men would be slammed shut. In their vision of society, the two cultures would have been one.

The enemy was monopoly. For centuries, knowledge of the soul had been shut up in the Latin Bible, which only black-coated ministers had to interpret. The administration of justice was monopolized by lawyers and judges, medicine by the College of Physicians. Was science now to be shut up in its own jargon, which only new specialists were to interpret?

Ironically, their vision of the democratization of science, and the widespread dissemination of knowledge, came during trying times, times when those in positions of power made moves to secure specialization in the hands of the few. The last of the polymaths were dying out, just when the radicals called for a mini-polymath in every parish.

Science as a worldview

Finally, the communicator of science must consider the aspect of science as worldview. By this we mean science as one of the most powerful influences shaping beliefs and attitudes to the Universe and man.

The conservative view of science is one that sees its laws as logical deductions from experimentally observed reality. If this were strictly true, science may never have developed. In actuality, the worldviews of science are based on more than mere facts. They are also reflections of the cultural milieu of the time, in which each and every scientist is unavoidably imbued.

So, the natural world is seen through many filters, social, political and cultural, as well as scientific. To take two prominent examples, Aristotle's geocentric cosmology developed out of the political crisis of the late classical Greek world, and Darwin's natural selection from the contemporary idea of the natural justice of free competition.

Once developed, these worldviews become paradigms within which scientists communicate solutions to certain puzzles. It can often be a question of disproving a theory, as much as proving one. The disproving of Aristotle's physics was the key to the progress of mechanics during the Scientific

Revolution, the proving of the theory of evolution crucial to the development of natural history in the nineteenth century.

Scientists are creatures of the culture in which they swim. Sometimes they swim against the stream. At these times, to advance the course of science and probe the secrets of nature, it is more of a question of overthrowing the established ideas of a given worldview.

Nonetheless, the course of science depends upon a continuous picture, one part science, one part society, which can be destroyed from time to time, and re-created in view of a new paradigm, based on the experience of the new conditions of science and society.

It's also possible to characterize the general way in which debates and controversies in science have been communicated throughout history. Since the very beginning of rational thought, there have been two opposing trends: idealism and materialism. Though the conflict between these tendencies is sometimes subtle, sometimes apparent, the social affinity of the opposing sides is quite clear.

Idealism is on the side of order. Its champion in ancient times was Plato, who argued that the truth was beyond question, and that those of inferior rank were not fit to understand the complexity of natural philosophy. Today's idealists argue the same thing in modern form. The aim of science, from this viewpoint, is to conserve, to explain the universe at large, and to suggest in elaborate and sophisticated ways that the sole purpose of communicating science is so that the public appreciate the status of science and scientists.

Materialism is practical and experimental. For centuries, the materialist view did not gain support in cultured circles, because of its revolutionary potential, the same potential that was realized in the Renaissance. It is fundamentally a philosophy of matter in motion, an account of nature and society from below rather than above. It is a philosophy that realizes the power of change through getting to know nature's ground rules.

Many debates in the history and development of science become clearer when we look at them from this viewpoint of a struggle between idealism and materialism. The idealist side is the side of 'order', and established religion. The materialist side shows both its power and its danger to established order.

In ancient times, Plato's idealism was in many ways a response to the Atomists, the material philosophy of those such as Democritus and Epicurus. In the Renaissance, the movement to develop a materialist and experimental science was up against its prime enemy of Platonic-Aristotelian philosophy, backed by the Church. And in the nineteenth century, the same opposition can be identified in the struggle between science and religion over Darwinian evolution.

The very continuation of the struggle, despite the successive advances of materialist science, suggests that it is not perhaps a philosophic one, but a reflection of political struggles in the scientific sphere. At various times, idealism has been used to justify an existing state of affairs. And at each stage, materialism has called upon a practical test of reality and on the necessity of change.

Perhaps the most recent example of idealism is the tendency towards genetically determinist arguments to explain human behaviour. Rather than focusing on the commonality of 99 per cent of our genes that we all share, much genetic research has targeted racial difference, and how variations in genes account for 'disparities' such as skin colour, intelligence or 'deviancy' in behaviour, a kind of Platonic idealism in modern eugenics.

Science–society interaction

This chapter has looked at the key features of science, as an institution, as a method, as a body of knowledge, as a key driver of the economy and as a worldview. This overview has been in the hope that it provides an introduction to the nature of science, and that such an introduction will help inform and contextualize the material in the remainder of this book.

Indeed, it is sincerely hoped that the content and context of this chapter are kept in mind, throughout the rest of the book. For it provides the backdrop to the developmental and contemporary interaction of science and society, and still determines the way in which the public engages with modern science. This certainly applies to the place of science in today's culture, whether it is the history and development of science writing, as with Chapter 4, or the evolution of science communication in popular culture, as with Chapter 2.

It applies equally to the principles and practice of presenting science in public. These are featured in chapters on event-based science communication, Chapter 5, the world of broadcast media, Chapter 5, and the history and development of science museums and other artefact-based communication centres, Chapter 7.

Finally, and perhaps most importantly, this introduction is crucial to the question of science and the citizen, presented in Chapter 3. For many, science has long been far too important to be left to the scientists, so Part I ends with a very appropriate overview of issues in citizen participation and the scientific enterprise.

References and further reading

Bauer, H. (1994), *Scientific Literacy and the Myth of Scientific Method,* University of Illinois Press, (Chicago).

Brecht, B. (1938) *Life of Galileo,* trans. J. Willett, ed. J. Willett and R. Manheim, 2001, Methuen (London).

Charles, D. (2005), *Between Genius and Genocide: The Tragedy of Fritz Haber, Father of Chemical Warfare,* (London).

Collins, H.M. and Pinch, T. (1998), *The Golem: What You Should Know About Science,* Cambridge University Press, (Cambridge).

Dowling, D.H. (1986), The Atomic Scientist: Machine or Moralist? *Science Fiction Studies,* 3(2) (July 1986), 139–147.

Dyson, F. (1984), Weapons and Hope Part II, *The New Yorker*, 13 Feb. 1984, 67–117.

Einstein, A. (1935), *The World As I See It,* J. Lane, (London).

Ginsberg, M. (1953), *The Idea of Progress,* Methuen, (London).

Gregory, J. and Miller, S. (1998), *Science in Public: Communication, Culture and Credibility,* Plenum, (New York).

Jones, R.F. (1951), *The Seventeenth Century,* Stanford University Press, (Stanford).

Jones, R.F. (1953), *The Triumph of English Language,* Stanford University Press, (Stanford).

Sprat, T. (1667), *The History of the Royal Society of London,* (London).

St Augustine, *Works,* ed. Marcus Dods (1870), T. & T. Clark, (Edinburgh).

Wells, H.G. (1898), *The War of the Worlds,* Heinemann, (London).

Wolpert, L. (2002), *Is Science Dangerous?* Nobel Symposium (NS 120): 'Virtual Museums and Public Understanding of Science and Culture', 26–29 May 2002, Stockholm, Sweden.

Science in Popular Culture

Neil Hook and Mark Brake

2

In this chapter we will examine the different approaches that television, film, literature, theatre and science fiction take to science. In the process we will examine the consequences for science communication using case studies to illustrate our thinking.

LEARNING POINTS

Theoretical learning points

- Science is a socially constructed culture.
- Science communication must be aware of the cultural context of its outreach.
- Different texts are not only perceived in different ways but can affect one another.

Practical learning points

- The metaphors of popular culture can make science come alive.
- Popular science can skew public perceptions.

Introduction

In the popular 'science faction' television show *Numbers*, the eminent (fictional) mathematician Charlie Epps helps his FBI Agent Brother Don to solve crimes with the application of mathematics. Time and again, Charlie seeks to illustrate his point with examples from daily life. He earnestly wants to communicate just how ubiquitous the use of mathematics is in our everyday world.

The assertions made by Charlie in convincing his brother about the value of mathematics can equally be applied to all branches of science. We all use science every day. Popular culture is filled with representations of the everyday; therefore popular culture is also full of science. You just have to know where to look.

The idea that science is something to be constrained in a laboratory is anathema to most scientists. They constantly talk about the application of their research. Yet when popular culture explores science, the scientific establishment is frequently sceptical. Even more so if one attempts to link popular culture and science.

BOX 2.1   WHAT IS CULTURE?

As early as the 1950s, Kroeber and Kluckhohn (1952) gave a set of 152 formal definitions of culture. Since then it has become increasingly difficult to provide a complete definition. Most people agree, however, that culture is a way of life that is handed on by each successive generation. This can include the arts, beliefs and institutions of a particular group. Recently, the United Nations Educational, Scientific and Cultural Organization (UNESCO) sought to describe culture by saying that ' culture should be regarded as the set of distinctive spiritual, material, intellectual and emotional features of society or a social group, and that it encompasses, in addition to art and literature, lifestyles, ways of living together, value systems, traditions and beliefs' (UNESCO 2001).

The respected academic Professor W.J.T. Mitchell whose background is in art history and literature published a controversial volume in 1998 entitled *The Last Dinosaur Book*. One of the assertions he made was that 'scholars who link science to culture are motivated mainly, I think, not by a desire to discredit science, but to understand it in a new way' (Mitchell 1998, 283). Mitchell uses dinosaur palaeontology as a case study to examine the way that popular culture and science interact. Arguing that the dinosaur is one of the pre-eminent pop culture icons, Mitchell identifies the need for a hybrid discipline which gives equal weight to both palaeontology and cultural studies in the future examination of these 'terrible lizards'.

Whilst Mitchell's call for a new discipline is ultimately flawed it does make a convincing case for a greater degree of cooperation and biculturalism between branches of science and other areas of academia. Whilst Mitchell does not go as far as the French academic Bruno Latour, his assertions provide us with some interesting conundrums: 'what place is there in science communication for a study of science and popular culture' and 'how as science communicators can we analyse popular culture?'

> ## BOX 2.2 BRUNO LATOUR (BORN 22 JUNE 1947, BEAUNE, FRANCE)
>
> This French sociologist of science is best known for his books *We Have Never Been Modern*, *Laboratory Life* and *Science in Action*. His prominence rose following the publication of *Laboratory Life: the Social Construction of Scientific Facts* (1979) which he wrote with Steve Woolgar. Together they produced a challenging and controversial picture of the sciences. They put forward the idea that the objects of scientific study are socially constructed within the laboratory. Latour and Woolgar claim that scientific ideas cannot exist outside of the instruments that measure them and the minds that interpret them. Together they see scientific activity as a set of beliefs, oral traditions and culturally specific practices. For them science is not a procedure or a set of principles but a culture.

The two cultures

The task of analysing popular culture has traditionally fallen to those within the humanities. This has led to an unhelpful bias against the study of the interactions between science and society as depicted in popular culture, a bias which stems partly from the idea of 'The Two Cultures'.

This was the title of an influential 1959 Rede Lecture by the successful novelist and scientist C.P. Snow. In it Snow argued that the breakdown of communication between the 'two cultures' of modern society (which he identified as the sciences and the humanities) was a major impediment to cracking the world's problems. Snow felt that with a foot in both camps he was ideally placed to render an opinion on this subject:

> A good many times I have been present at gatherings of people who, by the standards of the traditional culture, are thought highly educated and who have with considerable gusto been expressing their incredulity at the illiteracy of scientists. Once or twice I have been provoked and have asked the company how many of them could describe the Second Law of Thermodynamics. The response was cold: it was also negative. Yet I was asking something which is about the scientific equivalent of: have you read a work of Shakespeare's. (Snow 1960, 14–15)

Although similar concerns had been voiced earlier, it was Snow's work which made the biggest impact.

Snow's vision produced a major reaction in both academic and populist circles. This was in part due to the format of the presentation. As a lecture this clarion call was, impassioned not reasoned, inductive and (ironically) constructivist not empirical, and used rhetorical not evidence-based devices. In it Snow argues that the scientific worldview is embedded in society and culture, it functions as an observer making unbiased observations about nature.

However 'two cultures' soon became shorthand for the rift between scientists and intellectuals within the humanities/social science traditions. Although Snow backed away somewhat later on and argued that a third culture could emerge, at the time of the publication of his work he emphasized the inherent dualism of the debate.

Yet for all his much vaunted claims of being able to see both sides, Snow's 'two cultures' or to give it its full title *The Two Cultures and the Scientific Revolution* (1960) was mostly an articulate piece of popular science writing aimed at advancing the cause of science. In it those on the other side of the divide are largely characterized with antagonism and ignorance in the face of enlightened science. The ubiquity of his 'two cultures' phraseology soon came to eclipse the arguments and approach he deployed, so that it is still in use in popular culture today. Yet contemporary academics argue that the fracture of both science and the humanities into specializations, as well as the emergence of cross-cultural fields, makes two cultures seem ridiculous. It is argued that western society is much more divided than Snow's dualist model. Indeed some assert that Snow's approach caused more problems instead of eradicating them.

Snow believed the third culture would develop as a synthesis of the two opposing predecessors. However, John Brockman argued in the late 1990s in his work *The Third Culture* that there had emerged a type of scientist who attempted to directly interface with the public through popular communication. Instead of relying on the journalists and academics of the humanities to mediate their work for them, these figures are engaging the public directly. They are communicating science through print and especially through the visual media.

Science on television

The mission of television has been characterized as one that informs, educates and entertains. Its diversity and richness can at times be overwhelming as it depicts the wide varieties and disparate circumstances of human life. Yet frequent criticism is made of the way science is represented on television. All science seems to be presented as a conglomeration still representing Snow's singular scientific culture.

Frequently cited examples of this type of conglomeration of all the sciences into one monolithic structure include television news reporting in which the anchor begins a piece to camera with the earnest words 'Scientists have discovered'. Or perhaps the way that a visual shorthand has emerged in popular drama so that most scientists are characterized as wearing white coats and working with arcane equipment. Bennett (1998) talks of the 'passive translation' of scientific material via the telly boffin: an individual who is often called upon to champion and embrace all areas of science – he/she becoming the ubiquitous 'scientist'.

Science as portrayed on television can be characterized into two broad approaches. First the *obvious*; this includes television marketed as science (the documentary, the ethical piece, the weather) and this area tends to be dominated by 'nature' in all its splendid varieties. After all television is a visual medium and it is much easier to depict something that can be shown in glorious Technicolor rather than trying to convey abstract principles. Collins (1987) asserts that 'television presents science as producing unambiguous and intractable knowledge. The techniques used include re-enactments which telescope time and render work and skill invisible.'

The second approach is the *incidental*. Within this area we find that science is depicted in some form as part of the everyday interaction of the scientific method with the wider world. Thus we have the police procedural drama which ostensibly relies upon forensic scientists but in reality is about the human condition. We have the science fiction show which uses science as a way to place its heroes in jeopardy or haul them out of it. We have the show in which science is just a backdrop to whatever is the main event (vets in action, errant fathers identified by DNA test in front a baying studio audience or a politician critiqued for his handling of an agricultural crisis).

In this way television blurs the borderlines between fact and fiction. Dramas are often extrapolated from real cases with scientific involvement and studio debate shows sometimes present extrapolation as proven fact. This approach is not restricted to daytime television however. The relatively recent high-profile documentary *Walking with Dinosaurs* came under scrutiny for the way it presented scientific opinion as undisputed scientific fact.

BOX 2.3   CASE STUDY: THE CSI EFFECT

The 'CSI Effect' or 'CSI Syndrome' is drawn from the success of the television series *Crime Scene Investigation* in which science plays a core role in the depiction of a fictional narrative set amongst a group of forensic investigators.

The communication and glamorization of forensic science, necessary to convey a sense of drama, has purportedly skewed public perceptions of actual forensic science leading to a measurable effect on criminal justice systems.

In particular the depiction of forensic techniques as providing incontrovertible evidence has raised the efficacy of such techniques in the public's minds. DiFonzo and Stern (2007) point out that there is a strong link between misinterpreted forensic science and wrongful convictions.

Podlas (2006) identifies four main consequences of the communication of forensic science labelled as the 'CSI Effect': the creation of unreasonable expectations, an increase in prosecutorial burdens, the elevation of science to infallible status and an increase in public interest in the field of forensic science. Whilst the first three all cause problems in the courtroom it cannot be denied that the 'CSI Effect' has increased both public funding and career interest in the field of forensic science. The depiction of science and its communication via a narrative form has popularized what was once a backwater of science.

Whilst we can actually document large quantities of science depicted on television exactly how much of that can be labelled as *science communication* is up for debate. There are problems with science coverage on television. Not least because in its labelling of science, television tends to exclude technology as the application of scientific principles. Science is still depicted as a monolithic culture concerned with the discovery and application of abstract principles whilst engineering in all its forms, for example, is a trade.

Similarly television's depiction of science tends to exclude social science and its practitioners. It is not that they do not appear on television, more that they do not appear as scientists. The rigorous application of scientific principles as applied to work within the field of social science is often dismissed as being mere opinion or conjecture without evidence or methodology as a consequence of this failure. Thus the economist who has carefully tracked trends and markets to produce a well-respected piece of analysis is portrayed almost as a mystic reading tea leaves. This emphasis on the natural sciences as making up the field in its entirety seems to have one notable exception as far as television is concerned: psychology.

Psychology with its inherent appeal to the viewing public frequently gets a much wider coverage than other sciences. Partly this is because it is portrayed as an applied discipline. Its involvement in the scientific study of mental processes and behaviour often makes reference to the application of psychology to different areas of human activity, most commonly those related to everyday life (examples including family, education and employment). This not only creates recognition with the public but also allows for the more lurid circumstances of some peoples' lives to become prime-time viewing. Shows like the tabloid talk show hosted by Jerry Springer, amongst others, plays to this appeal. This also adds to the controversy surrounding the scientific nature of psychology itself with Thomas Kuhn arguing in his *The Structure of Scientific Revolutions* (1962) that psychology was in a pre-paradigm state, and as such lacked the necessary agreement on theory which had developed in areas like chemistry and physics. Criticism that psychology is pseudoscientific is not helped by having behaviour experts help us to monitor the contestants in *Big Brother* in the belief that we too could somehow inject our own analysis into what was effectively a scientific experiment (and is undoubtedly far more populist and popular than attempts like Megalab, to introduce the scientific method to the public at large).

At this point we should also briefly address the gender bias within television coverage of science. The debate over the role and promotion of women in science is both long and complex, and television has contributed to the debate in its own way. Generally speaking however, male scientists tend to be over-represented in *obvious* televisual science whereas there seems to be more balance in *incidental* (especially fictional) coverage. This could be due to the aspirational nature of most of the incidental coverage as opposed to the 'news value' dominated approach taken by the obvious coverage.

Global coverage of science on television also reveals that there is a profound anglospherical (English speaking) focus. Partly as a consequence of its own global promotion and also by virtue of its economic power, the United States of America in particular receives an out-of-proportion share of global scientific coverage. This could also be due to the role that American Global News Networks play in the dissemination of scientific coverage of an obvious nature. Thus scientists who work in other languages yet operate in the western context (for example Scandinavia) often find that the global coverage of their work is not penetrating as far as those operating within English. Similarly even within the anglosphere there is a bias away from developing countries and the contributions of their scientists towards those of prestigious institutions associated with large industrialized nations.

BOX 2.4   NEWS REPORTING

Often the coverage of science by the rolling news media seeks to expose scientific claims to critical analysis. This leads to conflict between that media and those engaged in research. Partly this is a question of expectation. Researchers expect a certain amount of deference towards their research and the time and robust nature of their methodology (even if deference is not in evidence towards them personally). This stands in contrast with the interrogatory tone taken by many within the news media. Partially this is due to the coverage of stories with a political angle in which the interviewee is expected to dissemble. The subjective nature of media coverage is at odds with the consumer's recognition of the infallibility of science. The viewer has been conditioned to expect interviewees to dissemble and fudge whereas they expect scientists to stick to the facts alone. The interviewer expects to have to dig at a pejorative 'truth' whereas the researcher seeks to present this truth up front. Similarly politicians are expected to extrapolate the consequences and applications of situations in an instant. This stands in contrast with the scientific practitioner who is far more circumspect about presenting theories without having had the opportunity to examine the data and their implications. Thus Collins (1987) reminds us that when the interviewer makes assertions and the scientist will not be drawn, 'the interviewer's contributions will appear more decisive than those of the scientists'.

Science in the cinema

When we consider the way science is presented within the cinema there are many questions which arise. How to convey science to the public? What messages *are* conveyed? How to react to these messages? What messages *should* be conveyed?

It is argued by some within the visual media that individual images are more powerful than narratives. A single shot of a burning child will tell more than any amount of voiceover explaining that child's anguish and pain. Cinema at its most basic is a visual medium which makes extensive use of metaphor to tell its stories. It contributes in a very significant manner to the formulation of public perceptions in a huge variety of areas including that of science.

Its popularity and social inclusiveness have made cinema a prime target for those who wish to popularize science. Numerous attempts have been made to engage the public with science by tapping into this rich cultural resource. Prominent amongst these have been books, documentaries and media articles which seek to explain 'the science behind.' (popular titles include Gresh and Weinberg's *The Science of Superheroes* (2003), Brake and Hook's *Futureworld* (2008) and Highfield's *The Science of Harry Potter* (2003)). Whilst these have had some limited success they have come up against significant problems.

The major problem is the restrictions of the medium. How, after all do you show a scientific breakthrough? Film is even more a surface medium than television is; the interaction with a film in the cinema is far less than television where we control volume, speed and colour. Our control of our home environment does not extend to the multiplex. We are far more likely to be submissive consumers in the cinema than we are in our own homes. Cultural norms require us to stay relatively quiet and passively accept whatever happens on the screen. The length of the film is set by the capacity of the audience to sit still and pay attention and unlike television you cannot easily divide your narrative into bite-sized chunks – instead you have to simplify, simplify, simplify. A science documentary series can often be spread over several one-hour episodes, all establishing the context of the topic and giving numerous examples, returning to points again and again to reinforce the central contentions. This is not possible with a cinematic format.

As a consequence movies tend to adopt stereotypes and visual clues with far more regularity than other visual media. The scientist is easily recognizable through setting, manner and clothes and the scientific process is reduced to an image on a monitor screen or a bubbling liquid being gently heated on a retort stand. These techniques aim to simplify the message (and consequently the science) to make it easier to convey within the constraints of the medium. A film is not the place for a piece of long exposition when every minute of screen time is measured in millions of dollars and the audience want to get to the next kiss/explosion/death/laugh.

Scientific meaning is drawn from the interpretation of verifiable data. Cinematic meaning, according to the great director and critic Eisenstein, is a juxtaposition of images, acting (performance), colour and music. This is why critics argue there are no such things as facts in a film. The notion of intertextuality (see below) is all important.

BOX 2.5   INTERTEXTUALITY

This is the shaping of texts' meanings by other texts. For example, an author might reference another text in plot, form, and style or even by direct allusion – thus some thrillers pay homage to Hitchcock in a certain scene or with a certain character. Similarly popular stories are often filmed several times, an example being the 2001 're-imagining' of *Planet of the Apes* by Tim Burton. Intertextuality also refers to the audience of a text referencing one text in the 'reading' of another, an example being audiences of the latest incarnations of the *James Bond* films starring Daniel Craig being conscious of the influence that the *Bourne* films starring Matt Damon have had on the depictions in the films. Another example would be the audience of a film being aware when watching the latest blockbuster of the previous roles that the star has already played, thus Marlon Brando's lacklustre performance in *The Island of Dr. Moreau* (1996) is instantly compared to his stellar performance in *The Godfather* (1972). The term 'intertextuality' was coined by the academic Julia Kristeva in 1969 and has since come to have a multi-layered and complex meaning with different academic fields adopting different variations of the central theme.

The notion of intertextuality asserts that all of the different 'readings', or ways of interpreting a film, combine to help the movie tell its story. A story has its own set of rules and does not communicate meaning in, for example, the way that a lecture would. Jung argued that these are the consequence of archetypes, structures and patterns embedded in our physiology and psyche which determine how we view the world. Critics like Northrop Frye and Joseph Campbell explore this approach, although for the student an accessible volume is Booker's *The Seven Basic Plots* (2004).

So movies translate scientific truths into a meaning which seeks to resonate with the audience. The director does this most often by linking the science being employed with the plot of the film so as to contextualize the topic. An example of this would be the way that director Roland Emmerich wrote and directed *The Day after Tomorrow (2004)*. In this eco disaster flick, Emmerich attached the scientific conjecture of global warming interfering with the ocean's thermohaline circulation to bring on a new ice age to a rescue story revolving around a father trying to save his son. Emmerich thus contextualizes the fate of the planet with a family and makes the story all the more accessible to the viewing public.

Directors do this because although expert to expert scientific communication has a common language, that of the scientific method, popular science communication has to both explain the science and highlight the connections to the cultural context of peoples' lives in a manner accessible and understandable to a lay audience. Telling a story is often the most effective way of doing this.

What this storytelling approach does however is create a paradox of credibility. The scientific community is trying to ensure that its discourse is both rigorous and meaningful whilst the figurative (entertainment) media are vague and ambiguous. Kirby (2003) argues that films act as a cultural barometer:

> fictional films play a role in the formation of consensus and closure in scientific controversies. The socially constructed nature of scientific knowledge means that scientists' knowledge claims only become 'facts' when consensus is reached. (Kirby 2003, 257)

Extending Latour's work, society becomes the laboratory in which science is socially constructed. It is only when society establishes a set of beliefs, traditions and culturally specific practices regarding a scientific endeavour that it becomes a scientific fact.

In other words, the context of the text is all important. A view which as we shall see is just as relevant in our discussions of the way that science interacts with the next of our subjects, literature. It is an awareness of this context that allows us to develop as effective science communicators.

Science in literature

> Literary fiction has seldom been seriously considered as a mode of science communication. (Russell 2007, 205)

There is a variety of ways to examine the relationship between literature and science. One could focus on the impact of science on literature, or conversely the impact of literature on science. One could examine how the two have an impact on each other. Some scholars have focused their examination on how both have responded to a common historical context. The development of literature has had as much of an impact on humanity's development, if not more so, than the development of science. The maturation of the way we impart information to each other, the way that we communicate essential truths as we have perceived them relies upon the development of narrative, of stories and upon literature in particular. We make such use of these stories that they become the common metaphors of daily life. Science communicators need to be aware of this issue if they are to utilize literature in their outreach work.

Before 700 BCE we have the domination of 'epics' and 'tales'. These narrative forms are usually based on either religious myth or some form of tribal legend. What is important to remember is that within these largely oral based forms the listener or reader assumes that there is a strong element of truth. In 700–400 BCE we see the emergence of three literary forms that introduced the idea of deliberate fabrication into the minds of both the storyteller and the audience. These three forms are poetry, drama and the 'philosophical discourse' (which contains elements of both of the former).

The domination of these forms continued until the end of the Pax Romana in fifth century CE. Much of the content of these narratives was then lost in the Dark Ages and only rediscovered (via Islamic translations and versions) by the crusaders some 600 years later. It was during this later period that medieval works (like that of Chaucer) started to emerge. In mid-1300s the *Decameron* by Giovanni Boccaccio appeared as the first proto-novel.

However from that beginning it took some time for the novel to emerge as the dominant form of literature. As literature developed it was in the early 1600s that the novel really started to grow (classic examples being Cervantes's *Don Quixote* in 1605 and Defoe's *Robinson Crusoe* in 1719). By the late eighteenth and early nineteenth centuries the novel had become the dominant literary form of the western world. In Britain we saw authors like Austen, the Brontes and Dickens become bestsellers. In France it was Dumas, Stendhal and Hugo, in Russia, Dostoyevsky, Tolstoy and Turgenev.

In 1843 Edgar Allan Poe wrote *The Gold Bug* the first whodunit in which the reader was *not* given a privileged point of view but had to wait with the characters till the end of the book for the solution to the mystery. Like science it followed a particular method in which hypothesis, investigation, evidence and then conclusions were drawn from a set problem. This was in distinction to previous works in which the reader was far more an observer than participant as they were allowed privileged insights into the plot. It is this idea of the reader as participant in the text (see the box on Intertextuality above) that is important when considering the question of science communication within literature.

Cartwright (2007) asserts that 'it is to be expected that the relationship between science and literature will largely be governed by the common historical and cultural context that shapes both activities' (Cartwright 2007, 116). Thus Chaucer and Dante mixed scientific terms unselfconsciously into their work because the distinction between art and science did not exist in its modern form. The way in which science is communicated in the novel therefore also depends upon the historical and cultural context in which that novel operates. Greenberg (1989) argues that

> when scientific ideas, images, and language appear in literary contexts – whether in novels by Dickens, Pynchon or Verne, or in poems by Milton or Donne – the original is inevitably transformed by being placed in a new context. This remains true regardless of the specific treatment of the science by the literary author or the intentions behind such acts of displacement or even overt appropriation. (124)

Thus even when we encounter literature in which the authorial intention is to be antagonistic to science or even complimentary, it is the context which makes all the difference. When considering science communication in literature it is *not* enough to just look at the texts themselves.

Is this just a way of excusing what Snow sees as the oppositional nature of the "two cultures"? After all isn't 'the aim of scientific rhetoric...to persuade us that it reflects only a world of objects; the aim of literature is to persuade us that it reflects a world of human speech, representations, actions' (Kipperman 1986, 77)? Here Kipperman argues that science and literature should not be reconciled as they are fundamentally different. He argues that science's quest for truth is apocalyptic – it seeks to reveal the absolute truth and strip away all conditionality. This stands in contradistinction with literature's quest for the truth, which is oneiric ('related to dreams or dreaming') – it emphasizes ambiguity and experience.

Paulson goes further when he argues that 'the successes of science as a strategy for knowing the world have taken intellectual territory and legitimacy away from literature' (Paulson 1990, 512). For Paulson literature seeks to persuade through believable narrative, persuasive rhetoric or the beauty of images and language, whereas science seeks to persuade by conducting experiments guided by sets of assumptions to which all assented, and then communicating empirical results throughout the community as plainly and directly as possible. These opposing methodologies for comprehending the world around us make the use of literature for science communication difficult. How does one communicate science using literature if it implicitly seems to reject the scientific method?

However, there are some commonalities between these two seemingly opposing approaches. They both use metaphor to address their subjects, just in different ways. Richmond (1984) argues that they are functionally interdependent on each other. He articulates a vision in which art is present as the creative imagination in science. For him art produces imaginary worlds, worlds which science tests using theories for their contact with reality. Science communication can make use of these imaginary worlds to establish non-threatening settings in which to explore and debate the science controversies of the time. In return for these imaginary worlds science prompts art to create new visions. Richmond looks to the work of Karl Popper who argues that when scientific discoveries are made new theories are discovered through creative acts of intuition. For Popper logic and rationality are only employed in the testing or criticism of the theory. It is this scientific rationality which is destructive as it seeks to destroy works of the imagination through testing and critique. By emphasizing the positive and constructive processes within, science communicators can raise the willingness of the public to interact with the scientific issues of the day.

As both scientists and science communicators therefore, we should be emphasizing the scientific use of creative intuition (imagination). It is this creative intuition which is constructive in that it presents novel ideas about reality as possible solutions to the problems of science. A classic example of this would be the work done by Conti and Conti (2003), who argue that science can influence literary creation and conversely literature can lend science credibility, and use the example of Claude Bernard (physiologist) and Emile Zola (novelist) as evidence. Inspired by Claude Bernard's *Introduction à la Médecine Expérimentale* (1865) Zola tried to adjust scientific principles in the process of observing society and interpreting it in fiction. Thus a novelist, who gathers and analyses documents and other material, takes part in scientific research. An example of this in Zola's work would be Zola's 1885 work *Germinal*, based on his extensive and rigorous research notes on labour conditions in the French coal mines – it was the first major work to address the issues of industrial action.

The interactions between science and literature and the incumbent science communication possibilities therein can be both positive and negative. The science communicator ignores our literary heritage at his/her peril. Far more than scientific analogy we use metaphors from literature to comprehend the world around us. Cartwright (2007) provides us with a handy list of the formats in which interactions between science and literature may take place. For the student of science communication this list can become a means by which an interest in science, and the communication of that science can be raised in non-traditional settings like literary festivals, mobile libraries, bookshops and even via social networking (see below). Cartwright's list reminds us that when we think about literature science can be deployed in the following ways:

1. Science as source of images, metaphors or explanatory devices.
2. Science derided, rejected or satirized (the foolish virtuosi).
3. Science as provoking cognitive dissonance requiring intellectual accommodation and negotiation.
4. Science celebrated – the scientists as hero, or science applauded as evidence of a Divine power.
5. Didactic verse – poems of science.
6. The Romantic dismissal – science as cold and inhuman.
7. Scientific irresponsibility – Faust, Frankenstein etc.

Cartwright does not come down on one side or the other as to whether literature or science has ontological primacy. Whilst recent develops in both fields have led to such claims being asserted it is best for the student to think carefully about using such stereotypes as they tend to create argument and debate. Within this context literary criticism takes its argument from the approach of 'science as text'. This posits that science is just another form of text and shouldn't occupy a privileged position (particularly advanced by the critic George Levine). The argument is made that one can use literary techniques to demystify science's discourse. A good example for the student to examine would be Gillian Beer's *Darwin's Plots* (1983) which looks at how Darwin's use of language shaped his narrative.

Literature is not alone however in its claims for ontological primacy. Within science the recent emergence of biopoetics (or Darwinian Literary Criticism), which seeks to apply Darwinian principles to the study of literature has introduced controversy. Biopoetics argues that literature can be viewed as a type of cognitive mapping. It claims that complex organisms construct a map of their physical and social environments to allow them to navigate their way though life. Literature introduces us to situations and concepts we have not encountered in person, resourcing us for future interactions. Michelle Sugiyama (2001) argues that a classic example would be the Cinderella type story (with its numerous cultural variants). This well-known 'fairy tale' is consistent with the work done by Daly and Wilson (1996) on homicide by step-parents. What is of interest is that the Cinderella tale has also made a very successful transition to one of the most populist forms (the pantomime) of the medium that we now move to examine: science on the stage.

Science on stage

Science is inherently dramatic – at least in the opinion of most scientists – because it deals with the new and unexpected. But does it follow that scientists are dramatic personae, or that science automatically becomes the stuff of drama? Djerassi (2007)

Silvana Barbacci (2004) identifies two possible connections between science and theatre; theatre which is used primarily as a way to convey scientific concepts and ideas and theatrical performance that draws its content from science while preserving its own features as an artistic expression. Magni (2002) points out there is a third, albeit slightly related connection which he refers to as *scientific theatre* by which he means the use of high-tech instruments such as micro-cameras or multimedia equipment for the scenery and direction, where the science is found 'backstage'.

Theatre is defined by Peter Brook in his 1968 classic *The Empty Space* as first of all, an encounter between the audience and the actors. Barbacci takes this as a starting point to extrapolate a six-point classification for performances combining science and theatre.

There is a marked difference between theatre used mainly to communicate science (the first two of Barbacci's classifications) and theatre maintaining its

---

BOX 2.6   BARBACCI'S CLASSIFICATION FOR PERFORMANCES COMBINING SCIENCE AND THEATRE (2004)

1. Theatre as a set of performing techniques to support didactics
2. Theatre deriving from the 'scientific conferences' tradition
3. Theatre posing ethical questions on the responsibility of science and scientists towards the society
4. Theatre pointing to existential reflection
5. Theatre staging either biographies of scientists or episodes from the history of science
6. Theatre using certain sciences (such as neurobiology, anthropology, anatomy, cognitive sciences) as a support for the artistic creation

characteristic of an artistic expression, drawing elements from the scientific universe to create drama (the latter four of Barbacci's classifications). Kirsten Shepherd-Barr (2006) argues that 'The most striking contribution of science plays is that the best ones successfully employ a particular scientific idea or concept as an extended metaphor. They literally enact the idea that they engage' (Shepherd-Barr 2006, 6).

When theatre is employed as overt science communication and as a means of supporting didactics (the theory of teaching and, in a wider sense, the theory and practical application of teaching and learning), the performing elements help to lower the barriers between an inexperienced public and scientific content. Some of these performing elements identified in Barbacci's work include the physical performance area, lighting and audio elements, the use of images, the 'dramatic vocabulary' of movement, the bodies of the performers participating and the verbal language which is being employed.

The main strengths of theatre as overt science communication are the ways that it can foster both emotional communication and sensory communication between the communicator and the audience. The pedagogical (teaching) activity is reconciled with the entertainment, the aim being to excite curiosity towards the scientific world.

Common examples of such activities include work done in museums, hands-on science centres, and science festivals, all of whom have an outreach mandate. Other examples could include occasional work done by scientific institutions, educational work in a formal (scholastic) context and presentations at scientific conferences (performances which Barbacci argues derive from the tradition of the 'scientific conferences', which started in the seventeenth century and coincide with the origin and rapid expansion of the original 'scientific Academies'). These groups sought to emphasize the 'marvellous' within science and were very popular as a form of mass entertainment amongst certain classes and audiences.

Yet when theatre is presented as science drama (drawing upon a motif of inspiration from science) a very different scenario is presented. This dramatic creation is inspired by science without any specific purpose of communicating its contents. Examples of this include theatre dealing with ethical issues generated by scientific discoveries, for example *Galileo's Life* by Bertolt Brecht, whose first revision, after the atomic bomb was dropped, was centred on the responsibility of scientists towards humanity. It can also be used to categorize theatre portraying episodes of famous scientists' lives, a frequently cited example of which would be Michael Frayn's *Copenhagen*.

Some theatrical activities draw on scientific ideas to support the creation of dramas. Science itself can provide technical input into the mechanics of drama. Not just lighting, sound and staging but also the use of neurophysiology, psychology, cognitive sciences, anthropology and anatomy to improve the actor's technique. Peter Brook, whose research examines the actor's performance in these areas, created two performances where such 'brain sciences' are the nucleus of the drama: Je suis un phénomène and L'homme qui....

BOX 2.7   SCIENCE THEATRE IN MUSEUMS AND SCIENCE CENTRES

Larry Gard when President of the International Theatre Alliance reflected on his experience as artistic director of the Carpenter Science Theater and produced some helpful points for those considering using theatre in science communication contexts like museums and science centres (Gard 2002):

1. Theatre creates a subjective reaction and relationship to the subject which can change from performance to performance – not every audience will react the same.
2. Material will need to be presented differently depending on the context – a museum gallery will be different to a bespoke stage in a science centre.
3. Literary merit must come first – it doesn't matter how accurate or innovative the science is, if the script is bad no one will stay beyond the first few minutes.
4. Good tools enhance the message – using experienced actors, directors and stage designers makes all the difference to the final product.
5. Quality should be measured and maintained – effective evaluative techniques can help in the development of future performances.

There are excellent examples of good quality productions in various venues; those considering use of theatre for science communication should look at their examples before commencing the development of their own piece.

Carl Djerassi, professor of Chemistry at Stanford University since 1959, has engaged in a trilogy of works that he defines as 'science within theatre'. He intends to 'explain science through a theatre in which science plays a protagonist not an ancillary role and where it is impeccably correct'. His first show, *An Immaculate Misconception* (2000), contains a live video describing the ICSI technique, which consists in injecting one spermatozoon into an ovum. The main theme is the conflict in modern society between the progress made by technology and the ethical quandaries it produces.

There are however critiques of science theatre. Paul Feyerabend in his work *The Theatre as an Instrument of the Criticism of Ideologies* (1967) claims that didactic works (that emphasize instruction and teaching) kill art and that they can only be written when everything has been learned. For Feyerabend, theatre is not a suitable medium to transmit ideas, it can only 'render them unrefined', which simplifies them in a dangerous manner, and trivializes or debases them. For Feyerabend theatre is based in subjective not objective truths, yet the work of Latour and Woolgar (see above) in turn challenges Feyerabend, reminding us that the social construction of all knowledge makes science theatre a valid means of communicating science.

It is the case however that when using theatre as a means to communicate science and ideas, epistemological (referring to something with relation to knowledge or belief) problems immediately arise. After all a debate on science cannot be conducted without giving (and having, more or less consciously) an image of it.

Science theatre can also be misunderstood, as it is often seen only as a marketing tool for the host institution or a product designed to generate publicity. This can lead to the accusation of theatre as rhetoric designed to be a superficial way of popularizing science. A similar accusation has been levied at the final subject we examine in this chapter: the way that science communication can examine the interactions between science and science fiction.

Science and science fiction

What is science fiction? Damon Knight's oft quoted definition that 'it means what we point to when we say it' (Knight 1967, 1), is very convenient but hardly robust. Many definitions abound including our own:

> science fiction logically extrapolates analytical scenarios from the crucible of science, but that is not its task. Its task is to inspire those reading to open their minds up to the inherent possibilities that exist within science. (Brake and Hook 2007, 253)

At its core, the perception of science fiction itself, revealed in how those who interface with it define science fiction, cuts to the heart of science communication. Those who dismiss science fiction as rocket ships and ray guns ignore its potential for bridging the divide between science and its publics. Similarly those who see science communication as simply opening the laboratory to visitors once a year or a necessary funding device, also ignore that same potential.

In order to see science fiction as a useful tool for science communication we must first examine it in a critical light and establish a methodology for it to be deployed in science communication. A useful analytical model can be drawn from the work of the important postmodern theorist Jean Baudrillard. In his 1981 text *Simulacres et simulation* Baudrillard identifies the traditional antonym split between Utopia (as good place) and Dystopia (as bad place) and extends it to also include Outopia (no place). Between these three then, we have both positive and negative visions of the impact of science as well as a way of cataloguing 'the other'.

Brian Martin's argument that 'most approaches to the study of science and technology only examine what exists, not what might exist in a different sort of society' (Martin 1997, 456) would seem to have some weight behind it. After all the flaw in such approaches is that they all 'have a conservative orientation, in that they affirm that which exists and offer no analytical means for focussing attention on what might exist in a different society' (Martin 1997,

456). Science fiction can provide the means by which the general public can participate in a consideration of those possibilities.

By extrapolating future scenarios we can map out the possible directions in which our own societies could develop, and seek to mitigate some of the concerns. As Weingart et al. remind us 'science is associated with the unknown future, and it becomes the object of projections of utopias and dystopias' (Weingart et al. 2003, 286). The general public are allowed to examine the possibilities through the use of science fiction. Science fiction becomes a methodology of extrapolation in a popular context. Martin comments that

> this method of comparing the actual development of science and technology in society with the likely development that would occur with a different set of policies or social organisation can be called a 'utopian' analysis of science and technology ... this method could also be carried out in the 'dystopian' mode, by imagining undesirable futures – such as a world fascist state – and the likely science and technology that would accompany it. (Martin 1997, 456–457)

Science fiction is a topic that stretches across film, television, literature and even the stage. As a consequence the comments made about all of the previous topics could easily apply to aspects of science fiction. It can play a role in the formation of controversy and help in establishing consensus views. If, as Latour maintains, scientific knowledge is socially constructed then we would argue that science fiction is hugely influential in that construction. However, it frequently plays an additional role, that of the social conscience of science and technology. As Felicity Mellor argues, 'science fiction is not, therefore, some "add-on" used simply to make science more digestible to the public. It plays a role in meaning-making both in the production of science and in the representation of science' (Mellor 2003, 519).

Much has been written about the communication of science in science fiction (Nicholls 1983; Bly 2005) although Lambourne does remind us that 'much that is sold under the banner of science fiction has little or nothing to do with science and is irrelevant to the study of science communication' (Lambourne 1998, 146). Nevertheless even Lambourne acknowledges that

> subtle examples of science communication in a fictional setting may concern the nature and purpose of science, the process of science, the character and experience of scientists, or the historical, political and sociological aspects of science, including its impacts on society. (146–147)

Weingart et al. (2003) refer to science fiction as the alter ego of science. Like Jekyll and Hyde there are two halves: the logical scientist engaging in rational laboratory style experiments or work in the field, alongside the wild-haired madman who keeps wailing on about the social consequences of these scientific discoveries.

The influential work of Haynes (1994) charts how the public's perceptions of science are influenced by the iconic stereotypes established about scientists, research which is supported by Frayling in his accessible book *Mad, Bad and Dangerous?: The Scientist and the Cinema* (2005).

Science fiction examines the expectations and anxieties of science. Weingart, Muhl and Pansegrau comment thus:

> If the position of science is as precarious as the myths suggest, it may be fruitful to explore the patterns and stereotypes that the popular media reproduce. They may reveal expectations and anxieties directed at science. Their continuity and intensity may indicate that the current criticisms of specific research lines (such as stem cell research) or certain technical projects (such as the genetic manipulation of food) are only manifestations of a much more profound ambivalence toward 'new knowledge', to the ever faster production of which our societies are committed. (Weingart et al. 2003, 281–282)

Indeed Robins (1999) uses a specific example when she asserts that science fiction has been particularly useful in allowing the public to access biotechnology debates around the future of cloning. Although the scientific community takes great care in making it clear that a future in which the wholesale cloning of humans is far off, the science fictional analogies produced for and consumed by the public have also identified substantial disquiet about the cloning of animals and other associated issues.

One vision of science fiction which has been a staple of our daily lives is the emergence of a widespread electronic forum in which the majority of humanity is connected, intangibly to the rest of the world. The issue of science communication on the Internet is discussed elsewhere in this volume. However there is one particular issue which in common with other issues in this chapter focuses around contributions from authors and the reactions of an audience – namely social networking.

Science communication and social networking

The development of what has been referred to as 'the participatory web' (Web 2.0) has led to a new iteration of popular culture focused on online networking via sites such as *Facebook, Twitter, MySpace* and *Bebo*. In the beginning of the development of such sites they were used by science communicators as ways of coordinating events based marketing and they can still be utilized in such a manner to great success, allowing communicators to inform individuals and organizations with similar interests of upcoming events. This is an extension of common interest groups which already exist establishing an online presence. With the introduction of virtual forums like *Second Life* the participative web became a venue in itself for such meetings with *Nature* amongst others taking full advantage of the facility.

The attraction of social networking is that it seems tailor-made for reaching out to 'non-traditional' audiences for science – non-traditional in the sense that one of the dominant features of social networking is the organic and non-structured way that users navigate the sites resulting in 'accidental' exposure to many topics science communication issues amongst them. It is also significant that those who have an interest, connection or knowledge of science often act as clearing houses for their extended network of contacts allowing information, activities and innovations to be recommended and endorsed by such informal opinion makers. Thus an individual who has both professional, private and enthusiast associates can quickly blur the lines which traditionally exist between such groups, transgressing boundaries and establishing an innovative network of recipients for science communication activities. When you add in additional features such as picture sharing via *Flickr* or videocasting via *YouTube* then the possibilities start to expand even further.

It would seem that the advantages to such innovation do not have any downside; the implicit participatory interface means that it is virtually impossible for a deficit model of science communication to be established. Any attempt to lock out user comments and replies normally results in either lack of traffic or violent flaming (online criticism) in other forums. Yet there are drawbacks for the science communication practitioner to consider: a static paradigm is not generally acceptable and considerable time and effort must normally be made to both establish a meaningful social network and maintain it. Secondly there are many social networking sites and decisions will have to be taken as to which one you will use, meaning that a specific audience will inevitably be targeted. Finally although the interfaces claim to be intuitive they are designed primarily for 'social' networking and *not* science communication – practitioners may find that the facilities on offer are not what they would want.

Conclusion

When considering science communication as a means of bridging the gap between science and culture we must take the work of Bruno Latour as our fundamental foundation. Science is a socially constructed culture and therefore science communication must always be aware of the cultural context of its outreach. The setting, staging and examples used in science communication all resonate with metaphors drawn from the public's interactions with stage, screen and literature. Properly used these links can dramatically raise the effectiveness of science communication activities. If ignored then the cultural context of a piece of science communication can skew the public's perceptions of the science being communicated in unexpected ways. No piece of communication exists in a vacuum, previous interactions can change the way the work is perceived.

Popular culture can be one of the most effective tools within the science communicators' toolbox; however, if ignored it can also be one of the most dangerous pitfalls.

ACTIVITIES

▦ Watch a cultural text (film, play, television) that has some scientific content and imagine how you could use that text in a piece of science communication to a specific group. Then repeat the exercise but vary the audience.

▦ Gather together a group of people (formally or informally) drawn from both sides of the 'two cultures' debate and recreate the controversy whilst documenting the responses.

▦ Identify and examine a classic piece of science fiction that has transitioned between different formats (book, film, television, play); compare and contrast the different techniques used to communicate the science involved. Identify which version you would use in different science communication activities.

References and further reading

Barbacci, S. (2004), *Science and Theatre: A Multifaceted Relationship between Pedagogical Purpose and Artistic Expression.* Paper presented at the 8th International Conference on Public Communication of Science and Technology, Barcelona.

Baudrillard, J. (1981), *Simulacres et simulation.* University of Michigan Press (Ann Arbour, MI).

Beer, G. (1983), *Darwin's Plots: Evolutionary Narrative in Darwin, George Eliot and Nineteenth-Century Fiction.* Cambridge University Press (Cambridge).

Bennett, J. (1998), Science on Television: A Coming of Age? in Scanlon et al. (eds), *Communicating Science: Contexts and Channels.* Routledge (London).

Bly, R.W. (2005), *The Science in Science Fiction.* BenBella Books (Dallas, TX).

Booker, C. (2004), *The Seven Basic Plots.* Continuum (London).

Brake, M. and Hook, N. (2007), *Different Engines: How Science Drives Fiction and Fiction Drives Science.* Macmillan Science (Basingstoke, Hampshire).

Brake, M. and Hook, N. (2008), *Futureworld: Where Science Fiction Becomes Science.* Boxtree (London).

Brockman, J. (1995), *Third Culture: Beyond the Scientific Revolution.* Touchstone Press.

Cartwright, J. (2007), Science and Literature: Towards a Conceptual Framework, *Science and Education* 16 (2), 115–139.

Collins, H.M. (1987), Certainty and the Public Understanding of Science: Science on Television, *Social Studies of Science* 17 (4) (November 1987), 689–713.

Conti, F. and Conti, S.I. (2003), On Science and Literature: A Lesson from the Emile-Zola Case, *Bioscience* 53 (9), 865–869.

Daly, M. and Wilson, M. (1996), Violence against Stepchildren, *Current Directions in Psychological Science* (Association for Psychological Science) 5 (3), 77–81.

DiFonzo, J.H. and Stern, R.C. (2007), Devil in a White Coat: The Temptation of Forensic Science in the age of CSI, *New England Law Review* 41, 503–532.

Djerassi, C. (2000), An *Immaculate Misconception: Sex in an Age of Mechanical Reproduction.* Imperial College Press (London).

Djerassi, C. (2007), When is 'Science on Stage' Really Science? *American Theatre* 24, 96–103.

Emmerich, R. (2004), *The Day After Tomorrow*. Twentieth Century Fox Film Corporation.

Feyerabend, P.K. (1967), The theatre as an Instrument of the Criticism of Ideologies – Notes on Ionesco, *Inquiry* 10 (1).

Frayling, C. (2005), *Mad, Bad and Dangerous? The Scientist and the Cinema*. Reaktion (London).

Gard, L. (2002), Carpenter Science Theatre, *Interdisciplinary Science Reviews* 27 (3), 163–165.

Greenberg, M.L. (1989), Afterword: Some Contexts for Literature and Science, *Studies in the Literary Imagination* 22 (1) (Spring), 199.

Gresh, L.H. and Weinberg, R. (2003), *The Science of Superheroes*. Wiley Press (Hoboken, NJ).

Haynes, R.D. (1994), *From Faust to Strangelove: Representations of the Scientist in Western Literature*. Johns Hopkins University Press (Baltimore).

Highfield, R. (2003), *The Science of Harry Potter*. Penguin (USA).

Kipperman, M. (1986), The Rhetorical Case against a Theory of Literature and Science, *Philosophy and Literature* 10 (1) (April), 76–83.

Kirby, D.A. (2003), Science Consultants, Fictional Films, and Scientific Practice, *Social Studies of Science* 33 (2) (April 2003), 231–268.

Knight, D. (1967), *In Search of Wonder*. Advent (Chicago).

Kristeva, J. (1969), Word, Dialogue and Novel, in Kristeva, J. and Moi, T. (eds), *The Kristeva Reader 1986*. Columbia University Press (New York).

Kroeber, A.L. and Kluckhohn, C. (1952), *Culture: A Critical Review of Concepts and Definitions*. Papers of the Peabody Museum of Harvard Archæology and Ethnology, Harvard University 42 (1). Museum Press (Cambridge, MA).

Kuhn, T. (1962), *The Structure of Scientific Revolutions*. University of Chicago Press (Chicago).

Lambourne, R. (1998), Science Fiction and the Communication of Science, in Scanlon et al. (eds), *Communicating Science: Contexts and Channels*. Routledge (London).

Latour, B. and Woolgar, S. (1979), *Laboratory Life: the Social Construction of Scientific Facts*. Princeton University Press (Princeton, NJ).

Magni, F.E. (2002), The Theatrical Communication of Science, *JCom – Journal of Science Communication* 01 (01) (March).

Martin, B. (1997), Science, Technology and Nonviolent Action: The Case for a Utopian Dimension in the Social Analysis of Science and Technology, *Social Studies of Science* 27 (1), 439–463.

Mellor, F. (2003), Between Fact and Fiction: Demarcating Science from Non-Science in Popular Physics Books, *Social Studies of Science* 33 (4), 509–538.

Mitchell, W.J.T. (1998), *The Last Dinosaur Book*. University of Chicago Press (Chicago).

Nicholls, P. (1983), *The Science in Science Fiction*. Knopf (New York).

Paulson, W. (1990), Closing the Circle: Science, Literature and the Passion of Matter, *New England Review* 12 (4) (Summer), 512–527.

Podlas, K. (2006), The CSI Effect: Exposing the Media Myth, *Fordham Intellectual Property and Media Law Journal* XVI, (Winter), 429–465.

Poe, E.A. (1843), *The Gold Bug*. Hesperus Press (London).

Richmond, S. (1984), The Interaction of Art and Science, *Leonardo* 17 (2), 81–86.

Robins, R. (1999), Public and Popular Representations of 'Frankenscience', *Social Studies of Science*, 29, 295–301.

Russell, N. (2007), Science and Scientists in Victorian and Edwardian Literary Novels, *Public Understanding of Science* 16 (2) 205–222.

Shepherd-Barr, K. (2006), *Science on Stage.* Princeton University Press.

Snow, C.P. (1960), *The Two Cultures and the Scientific Revolution.* Cambridge University Press (Cambridge).

Sugiyama, M.S. (2001), Narrative Theory and Function: Why Evolution Matters, *Philosophy and Literature* 25 (2), 233–250.

UNESCO (2001), *Universal Declaration on Cultural Diversity,*2 Nov. 2001, UNESCO Doc. 31C/Res 25, Annex 1.

Weingart, P., Muhl, C. and Pansegrau, P. (2003), *Of Power Maniacs and Unethical Geniuses: Science and Scientists in Fiction Film, Public Understanding of Science* 12 (3), 279–287.

Science and the Citizen

Clare Wilkinson

3

This chapter explores a range of issues raised by citizens' interactions with science and technology and how they may influence you as a science communicator. Firstly, it considers current attitudes towards science and the existing locations and channels via which people access scientific information, many of which are covered in this book. Secondly, it examines two key movements in recent decades that have sought to increase the general level of scientific understanding amongst citizens: 'science literacy' and 'public understanding of science'. Next, it moves on to assess the role of science education, considering that which is currently provided and criticisms that have been made of it. It explores the role that citizen's views are coming to play in scientific and technological policymaking, whereby a problem is identified, a policy formulated and a course of action taken. Finally, it turns to emerging questions raised by 'public engagement' strategies. Throughout this chapter theoretical content will be interspersed by practical case studies; key topics covered include:

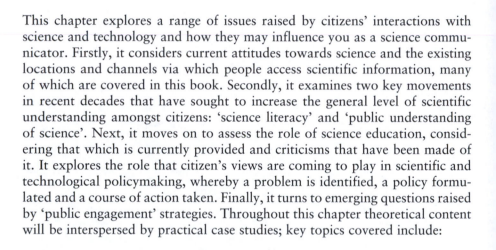

LEARNING POINTS

Theoretical learning points

- Attitudes to science
- Science literacy
- Public understanding of science
- Science education
- Public engagement with science

Practical learning points

- Developing survey tools
- Developing teaching resources
- Developing consensus conferences

Introduction

Many areas of science and technology have appeared controversial in recent years. Some of the most attention-grabbing and newsworthy science issues in the United Kingdom (UK) have surrounded developments such as genetically modified foods, new reproductive technologies and the global threat of issues associated with climate change. There is a long history of concern amongst citizens where new areas of science and technology are concerned, and the impacts that they may have in later years on the world, as we know it. The use and risks of nuclear power for example has long been debated. However, as scientific endeavours become increasingly sophisticated, raise new ethical or moral questions and are wrapped up in issues of risk and uncertainty about their possible impacts, it seems increasingly important that members of the public ask questions about them within societal settings.

In the 1990s, a sense of public and media distrust of science became more noticeable not only to scientists, but also to politicians seeking to reassure their voters, and to policymakers attempting to regulate new and emerging developments in science and technology. Questions were asked about how best to manage controversy, how to avoid citizen protests drawing a halt to potentially beneficial technologies and how to equip people with relevant information on which to base their opinions. Tied into this was a concern amongst some scientists that people appeared to be becoming distrustful and negative towards science. Many scientists became concerned that people would not be supportive of funding for scientific research or choose to go into scientific careers, at a time when from a practical and economic point of view, we are much more dependent on science and technology than ever before.

Attitudes to science

Surveys of public attitude

Recent data suggest people's views towards science and technology are relatively positive, despite frequent concern that people are distrustful or negative towards the fields. In the UK people's attitudes to science and technology have improved, since the late 1990s when mishandling of the BSE controversy and the introduction of genetically modified crops took their toll on public perceptions. In the most recent large-scale survey in the UK, published in 2008, 82 per cent of respondents agreed that they were 'amazed' by the achievements of science. In comparison, 75 per cent, still a relatively high number, felt the same way in 2000. Perhaps related to this increasingly positive view of science and technology, the data also show increases in people's interest levels. In 2007, 79 per cent of people agreed that we should take an interest in science, compared to 74 per cent in the year 2000.

When attitude surveys do find pessimism or concern amongst the public about science it is rarely due to negative attitudes towards science and technology per se, but is often about broader issues external to science or technology. For example, concerns might be expressed about how well an emerging area of science is being managed and whether the appropriate health and safety considerations are in place. Concerns may also be expressed about whether the science is being regulated properly. The public may question whether a technology is actually necessary or beneficial in the first place; perhaps they would prefer a non-technological solution to be found. Finally issues might be raised about motivations, particularly as science is becoming increasingly commercialized, with people asking who is paying for this and why? If public concerns emerge they tend to be about a very specific development or new technology, such as genetically modified crops, rather than about science and technology in general.

If we look to Europe we see a similar picture emerge. Most citizens in Europe are optimistic about the benefits of science and technology in general, but may have reservations about specific aspects of such developments, for example the environmental impacts of a particular technology. Likewise in the United States (US) people also report a general interest in science; over 80 per cent say they have some interest, but in comparison to other topical subjects, such as crime or health it does not rank particularly highly. In general, US citizens are thought to have more religious and moral objections to certain areas of science and technology than citizens of some other countries. For example, there has been widespread news coverage of the teaching of creationism in some US schools. Despite this Americans are positive regarding the benefits of science and technology in general, are supportive of governmental funding and are more confident in its regulation and leadership than some of their European counterparts. In Australia, citizens also largely believe that science and technology is improving our lives. Their concerns vary depending on the technology in question – wind farms for example are largely seen as positive, and attitudes to biotechnology have also improved considerably in recent years.

BOX 3.1   USEFUL SOURCES FOR ATTITUDINAL DATA

UK

Public Attitudes to Science 2008: A Survey, produced by People, Science and Policy Limited for RCUK/DIUS, is a good example of the UK's regular surveys of public views, available at http://www.rcuk.ac.uk/sis/pas.htm

Europe

The Public Opinion Analysis sector of the European Commission regularly commissions surveys and studies on Europeans, science and technology within its *Special Eurobarometer* reports, available at http://www.ec.europa.eu/public_opinion/index_en.htm

US

The National Science Board publishes its regular *Science and Engineering Indicators* which include information on US and international views, available at http://www.nsf.gov/statistics/seind08/

Australia

The Australian Centre for Emerging Technologies and Society produces the annual *Swinburne National Technology and Society Monitor*, available at http://www2.swinburne.edu.au/lss/acets/index.html. Biotechnology Australia has closely monitored public perceptions of biotechnology, available at http://www.biotechnology.gov.au/

From this information we can see that, despite some concerns, people are generally positive towards science and technology. What is less clear is how this translates into their knowledge of science or how they feel science is relevant to them. Citizen's factual knowledge of science and technology has been measured for many years now, not only in classrooms but in many of the same surveys of public views discussed above. These surveys often demonstrate that people have a relatively low to average factual knowledge where science is concerned. Perhaps unsurprisingly this often relates to their prior science education. Those that were good at science at school and continued to study science subjects for longer, appear to have not only a better recall for scientific information from their past but also have a greater versatility to learn about 'new' science topics, that would not have formed part of their earlier education.

Surveys such as these allow us to identify how science is perceived, to a degree, across the world, as well as to ask questions about specific technologies and people's views towards them, but they have their weaknesses. Often they are about capturing quantitative information, asking people to tick boxes and so forth. Where knowledge is concerned testing people in this way, some years on from their science education, may not be the most informative way to explore how people make sense of or understand science in their everyday contexts. Nor does asking very general questions about people's attitudes to science help us to unpick the very detailed ways in which people may come to be influenced or to perceive a specific area of science and technology.

Information on science and technology

Where do people access information on science and technology? We know the media still play a considerable role in access to information on science and technology, but that consumers can be quite critical of media coverage. Television, newspapers and the radio are key sites where people access scientific information; however, in countries where the Internet is widely available, its use as a source is increasing considerably.

Surveys of public attitudes to science coverage often demonstrate that people are very distrustful where the media is concerned. Citizens are much more distrusting of journalists than scientists, and they tend to have lower levels of trust in materials produced by the commercial media than any other source, including the government and church. Whilst people are sceptical of the motives of some journalists and media organizations, they are relatively satisfied with how science is presented via the media and the level of attention it gets in comparison to other topics, although they sometimes find science in the media difficult to understand.

The media is frequently criticized by the scientific community for its coverage of science. Journalists are sometimes criticized for their use of unreliable sources, and can also be seen as manipulative, distorting truth and debate amongst credible scientists. Criticisms levelled at the media include claims about inaccuracy, poor reporting, and how positively or negatively the science is reported. However, as we have seen in prior chapters the journalistic role is not always straightforward and journalists can operate within a number of practical constraints and with differing aims (see Nelkin 1995). These may not always be apparent to scientists reading or contributing to their stories.

In terms of the role of science centres and museums, public attendance remains relatively low in the UK and across Europe, compared to other types of attractions. Around a fifth of people in a recent UK survey reported a recent visit (within the past year) to a science centre and those who attend are often people who are actively interested in science. Science centres spend a considerable amount of their time in attracting young people and school students; here there is a wealth of often uncoordinated and anecdotal evidence that science centres have a role in terms of enthusing and educating people about science, but firm evidence is lacking in terms of how this occurs across the sector.

We can see then that in general most citizens are fairly positive about science and technology but that this may not necessarily increase the amount of information they want about science or how frequently they visit a science centre or museum. It is also clear from surveys that higher levels of scientific knowledge are associated with a greater interest and propensity to learn about new areas of science. How then have we attempted to make citizens more scientifically literate?

Scientific literacy

The context for scientific literacy

In the 1950s a movement was to emerge that would begin to address concerns at that time that the general population lacked an adequate level of scientific literacy. Scientific and technological status was playing a greater role in international competitiveness, particularly in developed countries such as the US. Scientific education and training however was focused on those students showing talent in science subjects, at the expense of the broader population.

Scientific literacy amongst larger numbers of young people was required to sustain the scientific and technological industries in which many developed countries had invested.

Although there were economic and political drivers for countries to increase their citizen's scientific literacy, there were also cultural and democratic incentives. In the mid-1960s in the UK, C.P. Snow described the emergence of 'two cultures' implying that there were fundamental differences between the scientific culture and artistic or literary culture. There was an anxiety that science curricula internationally were not adequately preparing all citizens for the new demands of modern life. As George DeBoer (2000, 586) describes it,

> Science teaching should still be for personal development and to help individuals adjust to life in modern society, but that world was changing. Explosive developments in technology and concerns about national security that arose following World War II were compelling enough to command a new approach to science education. The goals of science teaching for general education purposes within this new environment came to be called scientific literacy.

It was argued that a greater level of scientific literacy would encourage people to adopt rational thinking, to form arguments and collate evidence, useful in many practical areas of their daily lives. In addition, it was suggested that increasing people's scientific literacy levels would help them to identify the science and pseudoscience apparent around them, distinguishing perhaps between the predictions of a weather report in the newspaper and that of the horoscope pages.

Defining scientific literacy

Many countries across the world could see the benefits, both to the individual and society, in encouraging scientific literacy. But what exactly is scientific literacy and how did it come to be defined in this movement?

> The capacity to use scientific knowledge, to identify questions, and to draw evidence-based conclusions in order to understand and help make decisions about the natural world and the changes made to it through human activity. (The Organisation for Economic Co-Operation and Development's (OECD) Programme for International Student Assessment (PISA) http://www.pisa.oecd.org/)

> We would expect a scientifically literate person to be able to: appreciate and understand the impact of science and technology on everyday life; take informed personal decisions about things that involve science, such as health, diet, use of energy resources; read and understand the essential points of media reports about matters that involve science; reflect critically on the information included in, and (often more important) omitted from, such reports; and take part confidently in discussions with others about issues involving science. (Twenty-First Century Science – UK GCSE Science Course http://www.21stcenturyscience.org/)

Across the history of the scientific literacy movement, the term has been adapted and used in a variety of differing ways by different communities and educators. There is not then one specific definition in use, just as the term 'science' can be debated, but in general scientific literacy implies attention to three key areas of science:

- **Science content:** a level of understanding of scientific knowledge, facts and concepts.
- **Science methods:** a level of appreciation for scientific methods, practices and processes through which evidence is gathered and theories are validated.
- **Science within a social context:** a level of appreciation of the content and methods of science in order to understand, question and discuss science in everyday contexts.

Increasing people's abilities to grasp these three key areas helps them to become better citizens, and aspects of a scientific understanding have been steadily branded as 'citizenship' skills across the decades.

Criticisms of scientific literacy

Whilst at first glance it seems that a move to increase public literacy for any subject is a positive step, the science literacy movement has its critics. As the movement for a broader appreciation of science, its methods and contexts swept many countries there has been no resolute definition of what scientific literacy is, and its definition has varied across different countries and the sectors for which it is relevant.

Questions have been raised as to:

- What 'science' encompasses – should citizens be literate in all disciplinary areas? Or does a good level of understanding of biology, for example, compensate for a lower awareness of physics?
- Which of the three areas is of greatest significance – can a grasp of scientific 'facts', for example compensate for a low level of knowledge regarding scientific methods?
- At what level of knowledge is 'literacy' reached – are qualifications required? If so, to what level?
- At what level of knowledge should 'literacy' be maintained? How up-to-date does knowledge need to be, in particular as new knowledge develops all the time?

We can see that most of these questions revolve around how we measure 'scientific literacy'. And as we have already seen in our discussion of surveys, measuring the knowledge a person has is often much more straightforward, than things like their appreciation of scientific processes or the understanding they can demonstrate of science in contexts. As such, surveys of adult scientific literacy and assessment within science education has had to develop scales or related measures through which these three key areas of scientific literacy can be assessed within an individual.

The movement for scientific literacy, regardless of these criticisms, signalled a shift to the view that all citizens need to engage with scientific and techno-logical developments. Scientific understanding was no longer seen as a goal for the elite and talented few but as a minimum educational requirement for all. Scientific literacy was not focused on an improvement in educational stand-ards alone; it was acknowledged that adults and young people alike needed a basic level of scientific understanding to fully perform the role of a citizen.

Public understanding of science

The context for public understanding of science

In the mid-1980s the influential report the 'Public Understanding of Science' (also referred to as The 'Bodmer' Report) was published by The Royal Society. In a manner similar to calls for increased scientific literacy, the report's main emphasis was that public understanding of science should improve as coun-tries, specifically the UK, became more dependent on scientific and techno-logical developments. Understanding science was identified as part and parcel of being a citizen within a democracy that was more influenced by science than ever before. To make decisions, as a voter, on areas of science and technology, an adequate level of scientific understanding would be necessary.

In addition to the need for an increased level of general scientific under-standing amongst members of the public, the report highlighted the increasing need for scientists to communicate their work to the wider public. Particular emphasis was placed on communicating scientific research that raised novel questions or had an impact on citizen's lives, for example when residents live in close proximity to hazardous materials. The late 1980s was an influential period from a science communicator's perspective. The Committee for the Public Understanding of Science (COPUS) was created as a direct result of the Bodmer report. This committee highlighted that scientists had a duty to com-municate with the public, inspiring a broad range of science communication activities, as well as academic research into the field.

Public understanding of science and the deficit model

Although welcomed at that time, problems began to arise with certain methods and means used to communicate science within the public under-standing of science movement. An approach later known as the 'deficit model' underpinned many science communication initiatives of the time. The deficit model strongly implied that members of the public were deficient in their level of scientific knowledge and that increasing people's scientific understanding would benefit them, and most importantly, improve their view of science. This meant that scientists could, in a top-down way, provide members of the public with information. It was assumed that this process would then change their opinion of science and enable the public to come around (or up) to the scientist's way of thinking. This suggested that increasing public understanding of science would encourage support for science in future years. The movement suggested a disinterested and unsupportive group of citizens existed and yet, thinking back to the attitude surveys discussed earlier in this chapter, it is clear that it has rarely been identified to any significant extent.

Criticisms of public understanding of science

Many of the problems which came to be associated with activities under the public understanding of science banner centred on the three key concepts the movement embodied, alongside considerable criticism of the deficit model:

- **The public:** The initiatives emerging from science centres, science communication or scientific organizations at that time often reinforced the perception that scientists and members of the public were separate or different in some way. Instead of recognizing citizens as having a range of differing views, experience, understandings and perceptions of the role of science and technology within society, it prompted a homogenized view of the 'public' as one, unified group (see Irwin and Michael 2003). Scientists as experts were seen to hold all the cards and to have a superior role in some of the communication activities it inspired. In contrast to this view, research was beginning to demonstrate the role that citizens could play if they were dealt with in a more cooperative, respectful and participatory way (see Epstein 1996; Wynne 1996).
- **Understanding:** Like scientific literacy there was very little clear definition as to what level of understanding the public was expected to reach. In general, the movement for public understanding of science, focused on cognitive knowledge or the recollection and appreciation of scientific facts and concepts. Again, there were issues around how this increased knowledge could be measured or evaluated in the short and long term, particularly following one-off interventions and activities. There was also little clear evidence, ironically, of how greater understanding would increase support for science.
- **Science:** Attempts to encourage the public understanding of science often set boundaries around the 'science' to be discussed; scientists determined the areas about which the public were to be informed. When members of the public had genuine areas of interest or concern, questions that they wanted to ask, perhaps about broader moral or ethical issues, they could easily be labelled as irrelevant or poorly informed by scientific experts. Improving public understanding of science then for many scientists was a wolf in sheep's clothing. Instead of resulting in scientific support or literacy

in some cases it made people more distrusting of expertise, capable and confident of questioning and prying into scientific matters (Gregory and Miller 1998). For some scientists shepherded out of their labs into public activities for the first time, public scepticism rather than support was not something for which they were prepared.

Both the scientific literacy and public understanding of science movements have shared and noble goals. However, the loose emphasis on a general improvement in the public's understanding of science and the lack of clear definition of the scope for both movements made it possible for activities to be carried out under their guise which had a variety of other political, economic or individual motivations. By the late 1990s it was difficult to assess the impact the public understanding of science movement was having. Rather than widespread public support we saw controversy arising between scientists, the media and members of the public, as debates such as that around genetically modified crops, the MMR vaccine and mobile phone masts took hold in some countries. Many activities funded under the public understanding of science umbrella attracted members of the public who were already interested in science or motivated to participate, pointing once again to the significant role early experiences of science have in engaging people with science. It is then at this point that we shall turn to consider the role of science education more extensively.

Science education: building citizens

Formal science education – a global agenda

As we have seen, for a number of years there has been concern about the adequacy and level of the scientific understanding people have and attention has naturally turned to the science education sector, as the main provider of this underpinning scientific knowledge. A considerable driver for changes in science education is a sense that countries could in some ways become disadvantaged, economically and democratically, if they do not produce an adequate number of scientifically aware young people.

A recent UK report highlights current problems related to education that have implications for the science, engineering and mathematics base:

- A shortage of technical/practical skills.
- A decline in students (particularly female) taking up science subjects including physics, maths and chemistry, at A-level.
- A decline in undergraduate enrolment in chemistry, engineering and physical science degrees, despite the increase in admissions to science-based degrees taken as a whole.
- The low representation of women and ethnic minority groups in science and engineering jobs.

■ The lack of financial/workplace incentives for science and engineering careers.

In summing up these points, the report suggests that science communication activities may not have been reaching a large enough number of people to attract more people into scientific careers (Higher Education Directorate 2004). Again, the link is made between the role of informing the public about science and support for science, leading to the uptake of scientific careers.

This is a global issue; the Science and Technology Education Programme (STE) led by UNESCO suggests there could be impacts on global sustainable development and democratic decision making on topical science and technology issues, if sufficient levels of formal and non-formal science education are not provided for young people. The provision of adequate science education has been identified as influencing the strength of national economies and enhancing its citizen's employability, leading science education to expand internationally over recent decades. Issues affecting science education include low levels of understanding of basic science concepts and declining enrolment rates in advanced science education at university (see Millar et al. 2006, 19). This decline in enrolment, often for specific scientific subjects has been linked to student's attitudes and poor performance. The crucial facet here seems to be how subjects are taught, with poor quality and uninspiring teaching, combined with difficult compulsory curricula in earlier years, making science appear unappealing or inaccessible as a subject for many young people.

Globally, various educational interventions have sought to encourage a greater uptake of science subjects, and also to contribute to improving scientific literacy. Many governments around the world have sought to address these factors and the possible economic implications. The Australian government for example, has provided $38.8 million (approximately £19 million or €23 million) in a seven-year programme running until 2010–11 to develop scientific literacy and education initiatives. Its 'Boosting Innovation, Science, Technology and Mathematics Teaching' programme, which forms part of the 'Backing Australia's Ability' initiative aims to inspire 'more young people to take up careers that depend on excellence in science, technology and mathematics and building a culture of innovation' and is just one example of the type of political (and sometimes financial) backing these types of initiatives are achieving.

Performance and recruitment

Programme for International Student Assessment (PISA) (http://www.pisa.oecd.org) is an international survey of over 400,000 young people aged 15, and it provides a good indication of young people's proficiency in and attitudes to science-based subjects. Data from 2007 show that the highest performance in science subjects is amongst students from countries such as Finland, Hong Kong-China and Canada, with the UK ranking below countries such as Korea and Slovenia. Startlingly students in the US, a country with a strong science and technology sector, have a considerably lower level of proficiency than students in other industrialized and developed nations. The average performance of students in the US, in science-based subjects, is below that of countries such as the Czech Republic, Poland and Latvia.

Perhaps then motivation on the part of the student plays a role? And here PISA also provides some indications of the factors at play. Most young people surveyed, as in the attitude surveys discussed earlier, see science as important, but again this does not necessarily mean that they see it as relevant to their career options. Among the young people surveyed in PISA, 57 per cent said science was relevant to them personally and, in terms of career paths, 37 per cent said they would like to work in a career involving science. This suggests that at age 15 a considerable number of young people are still considering science as a possible career choice, and when the numbers of students graduating with science degrees at University is considered overall, this continues to be the case.

In 2004, of the 11 million students earning an undergraduate degree worldwide almost 4 million, just over one-third, were in a science or engineering subject. Breaking this down into regions the picture is similar. Approximately 38 per cent of UK, 38 per cent of European, 45 per cent of Asian, 34 per cent Middle Eastern, 32 per cent of New Zealand/Australian students earned degrees in science or engineering fields. Only slightly lower are students on the African and American continents both at 29 per cent respectively (see National Science Board 2008 http://www.nsf.gov/statistics/seind08/). However there has been concern that recruitment to science degrees is declining and some university departments in the UK have seen closures. Also it is important to remember that for many students an undergraduate degree may not lead them into a scientific career and that after university they may choose a career which does not use their scientific training.

The science curriculum

Like many countries around the world, science is taught as a compulsory subject in the UK and identified as a core component of education alongside English and Maths. Following the scientific literacy movement, science curricula have developed from an emphasis on facts and ideas to an inclusion of scientific processes and enquiry. There have been long-standing issues regarding the science education provided in the western world. In the UK the *Beyond 2000* report criticized the traditional focus of science education:

> Our view is that the form of science education we currently offer to young people is outmoded, and fundamentally is still a preparatory education for future scientists. An advanced technological society such as ours will always require a supply of well-qualified research scientists, but this requirement will be met, as at present, by

educating and training only a small minority of the population. On the other hand, the ever-growing importance of scientific issues in our daily lives demands a populace who have sufficient knowledge and understanding to follow science and scientific debates with interest, and to engage with the issues science and technology poses – both for them individually, and for our society as a whole. (Millar and Osborne 1998, 2001)

In addition to some UK-specific criticisms, common international problems in the provision of science education were also outlined by Millar and Osborne (1998, 2004–2006) in the report:

■ Scientific understanding, as provided by science education, does not equip students to translate their understanding of science into everyday contexts.
■ The sense of curiosity and inquisitiveness around science, which often appeals to younger children, is not maintained at secondary school where teenagers often lose interest in science.
■ An emphasis on knowledge and content can result in students losing sight of the bigger picture and the ability to make linkages and connections between ideas.
■ Teaching methods lack variety, with little emphasis on skills surrounding discussion or analysis.
■ Assessment is often focused on content-related activities, with a bias towards 'fact' recall, with methodological or scientific enquiry skills remaining difficult to assess.

Many countries have shifted to a scientific literacy model where by science education is compulsory to the age of 16, and additionally focused on producing informed citizens. Such a curriculum hopes to appeal to students by engaging with topical scientific issues that are of relevance or interest to them.

BOX 3.2   CASE STUDY 1: PROJECT 2061

The American Association for the Advancement of Science (AAAS) 'Project 2061' is a long-term project that attempts to address literacy in science, maths and technology. Project 2061 (http://www.project2061.org/) began in 1985, the year in which Halley's Comet was last visible from earth. The number 2061 refers to the year when Halley's Comet will next be visible and was selected as an end goal for the project which sets out to influence science education over a considerable and long-term period of time. The project has involved a variety of curriculum, teaching and assessment reforms. Particularly influential has been the creation of twelve benchmarks for scientific literacy: 'The Nature of Science', 'The Nature of Mathematics', 'The Nature of Technology', 'The Physical Setting', 'The Living Environment', 'The Human Organism', 'Human Society', 'The Designed World', 'The Mathematical World', 'Historical

Perspectives', 'Common Themes' and 'Habits of Mind'. These benchmark what children and young people should know about science, maths and technology from the ages of five to eighteen.

For example, a young person is expected to know and understand the following principle about 'the nature of science' and the 'scientific enterprise' by the time he/she reaches age 18.

Clear communication is an essential part of doing science. It enables scientists to inform others about their work, expose their ideas to criticism by other scientists, and stay informed about scientific discoveries around the world. (Project 2061, 2008)

Efforts at educational reform have been useful but despite identifying problems with existing science education, solutions remain elusive. Disagreement about the organization of curricula continues. Discussion rages about what should or should not be included within a science curriculum, from the simple perspective of how much room there is to add new content, to broader ideological questions about what is included or excluded in teaching. As well as the financial cost of developing and applying new curricula, there can be practical issues that only occur when curricula are translated into classroom practice. Teachers may lack confidence to teach new areas, lack sufficient resources or materials to support that teaching or feel burdened by a further pressure added to their workload.

A shift to focusing on scientific literacy for all has led to a considerable debate over the aims of science education. Those students who may have traditionally performed well in science subjects, or who are looking to enter scientific careers, are provided with curricula designed to match a broader and more general scientific literacy and may be criticized by some academics or future employers for failing to gather the basic skills or 'facts' necessary for a scientific career. Others argue that this claim is exaggerated and that the data demonstrate that students moving on from scientific education to jobs requiring specialist scientific skills are well matched in terms of numbers, with many science graduates required to enter more generic job roles (Osborne 2000).

Changes to pre-university education have implications when students educated within new curricula reach university. Higher education in general has expanded. Widening participation has been encouraged with the aim of attracting more students into university and from a more diverse range of backgrounds. Undergraduate science teaching has to cope with a more diverse student body while still developing future scientists, although it has been argued that much of the specialized scientific training now occurs at postgraduate levels. In addition, universities need to help students who may not enter scientific careers develop more general skills of appeal to a wider range of employers. Undergraduate teaching methods have changed to include more group interaction, collaboration and hands-on laboratory work.

Science for all?

As we have seen there are a broad range of issues affecting science curricula and how science is taught to students, but there are also issues that are specific to certain groups within society, such as ethnic minority groups and women. Differences in how young men and women are taught do not affect science and technology-based subjects alone, but the need to attract more people into scientific careers has highlighted this issue particularly in science education. In both developed and developing countries governments are concerned that neglecting female talent will reduce the workforce needed for economic and technological development.

Research shows that young women perform as well as young men in science subjects when the circumstances are right for them; in fact they can be very committed to science subjects as their education progresses, but the majority fail to move into scientific careers. While the number of women gaining science degrees has risen and is now comparable to that of men, fewer women enter scientific careers. Why do women reject scientific careers? Research points to a range of different factors:

- **Gender stereotypes and socialization in science and technology:** Like many other careers young women hoping to enter scientific careers lack role models. Fewer women teach science-based subjects in secondary schools and young women are not socialized with skills that are seen as 'scientific'. Skills, such as being competitive or analytical, are often masculinized and stereotyped as male traits.
- **Teaching methods:** Teaching materials are not always gender (or ethnicity) aware, they may not for example use female scientists as examples or consider learning methods that appeal to many young women. Collaboration, for instance, is seen as a more 'female friendly' teaching method than challenge. In the UK students specialize by subject in secondary school and subjects like physics and chemistry tend to be less popular with young women. In the UK young women are less likely to take single science subjects in secondary school and as such there is a less obvious route into university courses that may lead to scientific careers.
- **Career prospects:** The demands of a career in science are sometimes represented as being incompatible with choices young women may like to make later in life. For example, taking a break to have a child is a common reason given for the lack of women at the higher levels of scientific careers. At a more practical level, where more vocational courses exist women are often channelled towards traditional options such as secretarial courses, and gender bias in earlier education may mean that women do not have the subject-specific knowledge and skills for science-based vocational programmes.

Approaches to create more inclusive science education for young women have been criticized as an 'add women and stir' approach (Rosser 1997). Science teaching itself is seen as objective, and many strategies seek to add on to existing delivery. However, simply increasing the numbers of female students and their performance to 'male' standards, introducing opportunities like assertiveness training, or, the occasional female awarding the Nobel prize are all seen as quick fixes to a much bigger problem, which is about the way in which science curricula are delivered and their cultural or social setting (see Rosser 1997 for a critical discussion of some 'female-friendly' approaches). Instead, as Rosser (1997) recommends, there should be six stages to transform science education so that it is more inclusive for women, including challenging learning styles, recognizing the role that women have played in science and demolishing the perception that women are the 'problem'. This would lead to greater equality in what is provided for female students rather than simply expecting women to increase their performance. We know that female students are able to perform as well as male students; it is broader structural issues in how science education is taught that requires wider curriculum renovation.

Formal versus informal education

What role is there for science communicators to support learning about and interest in science? Science communication does not occur in isolation to that which occurs in formal science education settings, and as we have seen in the earlier attitudinal data, education seems to play a key role in both the ability and enthusiasm to participate in informal science learning later in life. There may be an educational element to many science communicators' projects and thinking about ways to develop creative, innovative and inspiring activities that support young people whilst in education and continue that interest in science later in life appeals to many science communicators.

Engagement: participating citizens

Introducing dialogue, participation and engagement

As we have seen there have been a number of problems with some of the earlier approaches to science communication from a policy perspective, particularly those which took a 'deficit' approach to the public as they attempted to encourage public understanding. In general many of these problems have centred on the lack of clear definition of concepts including 'public', 'understanding', 'literacy' or 'science' but it also involves the temptation to create catch-all groupings of the public, which ignores the significant variations there can be in how people learn, perceive or understand different fields of science.

In 2000 The House of Lords Select Committee on Science and Technology published an influential report, *Science and Society*. This followed a decade of controversy in the UK concerning issues such as BSE and genetically modified organisms, where despite the shift to encourage public understanding of science, there had been significant media and public dissatisfaction with the handling of scientific knowledge and developments. This report suggested that public support for science was polarized but that it could be salvaged before the public became anti-science. Importantly, it stressed that the public had lost confidence when it came to the regulation of science and technology. The report emphasized the need for 'better, stronger, clearer ways of science and people communicating' encouraging more open and positive communication. Drawing attention to these issues provided an opportunity to pivotally change and examine science communication and suggested there may be more transparent ways of consulting and communicating with the public, though there is still a presumption that this will lead to a greater appreciation of science.

In the years that have followed, science policymakers, scientists, the private sector and a variety of learned institutions have aimed to be more deliberative and inclusive in their approaches to communicating, particularly in European contexts. This has involved consulting with the public more frequently and speaking to a broad variety of people. Methods such as citizen juries, consensus conferences, Internet dialogues and science cafes are just some of the means that are being promoted to achieve a more two-way discussion with citizens about topical scientific issues.

Initially, in the UK especially, a good deal of this talk was framed by the word 'dialogue' suggesting a much more two-way approach to communication between citizens and scientists or policymakers. In recent years however, the focus in the UK has strongly shifted to an 'engagement' agenda, as we can see in a recent speech by Ian Pearson (2007, 1), Minister of State for Science and Innovation at the time of the speech:

> Difficult issues like nuclear energy and genetic modification have not been handled well. But there have been successes – our approach to engaging the public in the development of stem cell research in the UK has allowed this country to lead the world. The dialogue on nanoscience has generally been positive. We have all learned lessons. Public engagement is becoming recognised as a valuable part of policymaking....But we are only beginning to use the new tools of the 21st century for communicating with the public, like internet phones, blogs and deliberative events alongside the traditional mainstays of printed media, consultation and surveys. And in today's citizen centric world the value of a two-way process of developing and communicating our science policies with the public cannot be underestimated.

This statement outlines a considerable number of objectives for public engagement strategies. It seems positive and upbeat but the governmental emphasis on engagement has often lacked practical examples as to how more two-way approaches work. As such, in recent years, numerous people and organizations have sought to create, provide and develop practical examples and strategies to communicate with members of the public, many of which are innovative or have been evaluated to measure their success. In 2008, the commitment to engagement within a UK context was solidified by the launch of the largest ever initiative to support public engagement in the UK. Funded by HEFCE (The Higher Education Funding Council for England) and RCUK (Research Councils United Kingdom – a partnership of the seven research councils funding research into science, the environment, medicine, the arts, and social sciences), six 'Beacons for Public Engagement', along with a coordinating centre, have been formed to create a more structured and synchronized approach to public engagement in the UK.

The ideology of public engagement

There is a long history of public engagement approaches in fields such as healthcare, the environment and local government. Public engagement with science has drawn on this experience to develop a set of core principles, many of which are very similar to those underlying scientific literacy and public understanding of science models. Approaches for 'Citizen Engagement' now play a key role in most public policy settings (see Horlick-Jones et al. 2007. Some key motivations include:

- **Political:** There is a strong democratic incentive, that all citizens should be able to contribute to decisions that are likely to have an impact on their lives and become involved in the decision making process. Engaging the public has been most clearly promoted under the New Labour government since the late 1990s in the UK, despite concern that people are now less involved in politics generally.
- **Pragmatic:** Exploring and anticipating any public caution, concern or criticism could be useful if and when it allows scientists to avoid or prepare for controversy, particularly when significant research and financial investment in a field is occurring.
- **Utilitarian:** A number of studies in recent years have highlighted how useful public or local knowledge can be in creating socially robust knowledge or research. For example, in healthcare, service user or patient perspectives are now routinely sought for both long-term and occasional conditions.

There are practical issues in devising these types of activities; they can be time-consuming, expensive and require more involvement or commitment than a more one-way approach to communicating with citizens. There is often little practical guidance about what engagement is or involves and evaluation of public engagement initiatives has sometimes been incidental or poorly publicized to those who may find it useful. Engagement approaches have also been used when in fact a more one-way approach seeking a lower level of citizen participation is appropriate. It is important that public engagement efforts are truly that and are not a cynical re-branding of a more information-based approach. If a lecture is a lecture it should be stated as such, and not described as a science café.

Consensus conferences

Consensus conferences emerged in the 1980s in Denmark as a tool for engagement, and were taken up in many countries in the years following. A consensus conference involves three panels of people:

Citizen (non-expert group sampled from population)
Expert (those with expertise on all areas of relevance to the topic)
Advisory (representing a range of perspectives on the topic)

In addition, the media, policymakers and/or politicians may be invited to the conference to listen to the consensus views expressed. The advisory panel plan and support both citizens and experts as the conference develops and facilitators make sure that the consensus conference is held in an appropriate and democratic manner, so that the voices of both citizens and experts are heard.

The format of a consensus conference may vary but would normally follow a pattern such as shown in Table 3.1.

Table 3.1 Example consensus conference format

Panel	Timing*	Purpose	Outcome	Attendees
▪ Citizen	Days 1/2	Introduction of Topic Area	▪ Questions for the conference will be identified by citizen panel ▪ Relevant experts required for information will be identified and invited	▪ Advisory Panel** ▪ Facilitators
▪ Citizen ▪ Expert	Days 3/4	Question answering	▪ The selected experts will present responses to the conference questions established by the citizen panel	▪ Advisory Panel ▪ Facilitators
▪ Citizen ▪ Expert	Days 3/4	Discussion	▪ Citizens will ask for any clarifications from experts ▪ Citizens and experts will engage in discussion about that which has been presented	▪ Advisory Panel ▪ Facilitators

Continued

Table 3.1 Continued

▪ Citizen	Day 5	Discussion	▪ Citizens discuss that which they have heard together ▪ Citizens identify consensus (agreement) on views amongst themselves to the questions they initially posed ▪ Citizens document consensus views expressed by the panel	▪ Advisory Panel ▪ Facilitators
▪ Citizen ▪ Expert	Day 6	Presenting consensus	▪ Citizens read or report on consensus views ▪ Experts may address error or misunderstanding where relevant	▪ Advisory Panel ▪ Facilitators ▪ Media ▪ Policymakers ▪ Politicians ▪ Audience

Notes: *Timings are given as an indication throughout. They may be longer or shorter depending on the nature of the topic and involve periods of time in between for preparation or reflection. The introduction to the topic for example may be held over consecutive weekends before the actual conference.

**Attendees are given as an indication throughout. They may be broader or more restricted as appropriate.

A new term to emerge within science communication is 'upstream engagement'. Upstream engagement refers to a process of involving the public in decisions about very early stage research. The term 'upstream' refers to new and emerging science, where applications may not yet have been identified. Fields such as nanotechnologies and face transplantation are developing rapidly but are largely unfamiliar to non-experts. Involving people, while the science is still emerging, allows citizens' views to influence decisions made on the direction of research and development. This may help avoid significant research expenditure on innovations which are later rejected by the public. Questions have been raised as to how such novel developments can become visible to citizens, particularly when their applications or implications may remain very uncertain, and how (or if) citizens might come to really influence the research that is occurring (see Rogers-Hayden and Pidgeon 2007).

Whether focused on newly emergent science or more established technologies, public engagement activities that aim to be more open and consultative should not rely solely on expert advice or allow technical detail and information to overwhelm participants. Nor should they easily exclude any individual's views. A difficult balance must be struck that facilitates participation by scientists whilst also encouraging citizens to frame and present ideas for discussion that may appear too broad or even irrelevant from the scientist's perspective.

The role of scientists

Individual scientists may be uncertain or wary about opening up issues for public comment and debate, particularly given that some areas of science and technology have been met with considerable media or public resistance. In an engagement setting, where members of the public are encouraged to have a more participatory role, a scientist may have less opportunity to control proceedings compared with more traditional settings. There is less opportunity to ignore that which the 'audience' draws attention to or questions, or to control the direction of discussion. However, for a scientist working in a particular field, this can have significant benefits in terms of building knowledge of how an area of science and technology may be received or suited to members of the public.

A report in 2006 by the Royal Society (http://royalsociety.org/), *Factors Affecting Science Communication: A Survey of Scientists and Engineers*, suggests that many scientists see public engagement as a strategy to increase information about science and its relevance and benefit to citizens. In essence some scientists see public engagement as a means of enhancing the reputation of science and an opportunity to promote the positive contribution of their disciplines. Although some scientists acknowledged that public engagement provided an opportunity to listen and understand the public, when asked to define public engagement in their own words over a third of respondents described it as a method to promote public understanding of science. For most scientists, a lack of familiarity with terminology in the science communication field is likely to be at the heart of this response but it does highlight an important point. The aims of any public engagement activity should be clarified upfront for all participants. If the activity seeks to educate the public then it should be made clear. If the activity is about engaging the public with a specific area of science and technology, then the expectation of all parties involved, whether scientist or citizen, should be clarified and the objectives understood.

Some scientists may feel defensive of their expertise, after all they have often spent many years furthering their experience and knowledge, or they may lack confidence in communicating in a more participatory or two-way setting when used to more traditional approaches. However, in the above study, this was rarely mentioned, possibly because scientists relate communication to their 'teaching' experience. Time away from research, the lack of financial rewards, and negative impacts on career were mentioned as the main disincentives for scientists to participate and three quarters of those surveyed had received no media, communications or public engagement training.

Problematizing public engagement

In some of the announcements surrounding public engagement with science we can begin to identify similarities with issues that were also apparent with the science literacy and public understanding of science models. As such it is important that when you develop or contribute to a public engagement initiative you consider these issues:

- **The cohesion issue:** How do public engagement strategies draw together scientists and citizens? Public engagement must avoid suggesting there are inherent differences in thinking between scientists and members of the public, must recognize conflicting agendas and must avoid identifying citizen's views as a problem to be navigated.
- **The consensus issue:** How does public engagement recognize diverging as well as converging views? Public engagement strategies seek to provide more sophisticated, complex representations of citizen's opinions, and these may not always reach a consensus nor will it always be possible to represent these views in a numerical form. Engagement brings new responsibilities to the citizens that are involved, to be 'representative', and to contribute to processes that are still encountering practical and ideological challenges (Irwin 2001).
- **The expertise issue:** How does public engagement tackle the new questions it raises around 'expertise'? What responsibilities are placed on citizens in these interactions? There has been vocal academic debate concerning how our conceptions of what expertise is may (or may not) be challenged by modern science and technology, and the interplay of science and society that surrounds it (see Collins and Evans 2007).
- **The public relations issue:** How does public engagement resolve conflicting aims that may exist between scientist and citizen participants? Public engagement strategies must negotiate conflicting aims, facilitating citizen's participation where science is concerned but also in some cases encouraging public trust, confidence and support for science in a transparent way.
- **The 'translation' issue:** How does public engagement effectively feed into the policy process? (See Horlick-Jones et al. 2007). Although there is some suggestion that policymakers are now more attentive to social science perspectives (Irwin 2001), policymakers may be more open to traditional, quantifiable measures of opinion and may not appreciate innovative methods or represent qualitative findings appropriately.

A good deal of the public engagement work currently ongoing has occurred within public policy settings; it is less clear how such methods might integrate into commercial or industrial settings where issues of profit, confidentiality and patent are much more obvious.

Conclusion

Most science communicators work with citizens, in a range of capacities throughout their careers. Exploring how attitudes are formed and finding that many share an optimistic, if sometimes differently informed, outlook provides a useful foundation on which to base interactions. From a broader perspective, policy incentives for scientific literacy, public understanding of science and public engagement may not have an obvious impact on those frequent interactions with members of the public, citizens and audiences but undoubtedly influence how receptive certain groups are to science communication. As science communicators, understanding the reforms and incentives for current educational provision and science communication activities can not only be valuable for tapping into the formal education agenda and providing a perspective on how young people, the scientists of the future, are developing their insights but also help us to formulate effective and meaningful projects.

ACTIVITIES

1: Developing survey tools

Surveys are an effective way to quantitatively examine a sample of the population about their views, behaviour and attitudes. Surveys take a planned format, often involving the completion of a questionnaire or structured interview. They include a series of mostly closed questions from which people may select one or more answer, either in writing on a questionnaire or by telling their response to an interviewer who is completing a structured interview with them.

Think about how you could develop a survey tool that would measure the impact of science centres on their visitors (see Chapter 7). Consider the following:

- What types of background information would it be useful to find out on the people who are visiting?
- Which types of information might science centres be interested in finding out about their visitors? How could you ask questions about these?
- How could you recruit people to participate in the survey? When would the survey need to be carried out?
- What would be the strengths and weaknesses of using a survey method?

2: Developing teaching resources

Looking back to the case study on Project 2061 on page 64 think about how you could design a teaching resource which would aim to communicate to 8 to 11-year olds that 'clear communication is an essential part of doing science'.

- Which sorts of topics in science and technology might make a good example to achieve one of the benchmarks above?

▨ How could you develop a medium through which to communicate that (worksheets, games, lesson plans ...)?

▨ What could you make appealing about this to 8–11 year olds?

3: Developing consensus conferences

Referring back to page 70 think about how you would develop a consensus conference.

▨ What sorts of emerging areas of science and technology would make a good topic for a consensus conference?

▨ Which types of practical considerations would need to be made (materials, location, facilities, timing ...)?

▨ How could you recruit people to participate? What types of people should it involve?

References and further reading

Collins, H. and Evans, R. (2007), *Rethinking Expertise*. University of Chicago Press (Chicago).

DeBoer, G.E. (2000), Scientific Literacy: Another Look at Its Historical and Contemporary Meanings and Its Relationship to Science Education Reform, *Journal of Research in Science Teaching* 37 (6), 582–601.

Epstein, S. (1996), *Impure Science, AIDS, Activism and the Politics of Knowledge*. University of California Press (Berkeley).

Gregory, J. and Miller, S. (1998), *Science in Public, Communication, Culture and Credibility*. Perseus Publishing (Cambridge, MA).

Higher Education Directorate (2004), *Report on the Science, Technology, Engineering and Mathematics (STEM) Mapping Review: Volume Two*. 1–34, Department for Education and Skills (London).

Horlick-Jones, T., Rowe, G. and Walls, J. (2007), Citizen Engagement Processes as Information Systems: The Role of Knowledge and the Concept of Translation Quality, *Public Understanding of Science* 16 (3), 259–278.

Irwin, A. (2001), Constructing the Scientific Citizen: Science and Democracy in Biosciences, *Public Understanding of Science* 10 (1), 1–18.

Irwin, A. and Michael, M. (2003), *Science, Social Theory and Public Knowledge*. Open University Press (Maidenhead).

Millar, R. and Osborne, J. (1998), *Beyond 2000: Science Education for the Future, 2001–2032*. School of Education, Kings College (London).

Millar, R., Leach, J., Osborne, J. and Ratcliffe, M. (2006), Research and Practice in Education, in Millar, R., Leach, J., Osborne, J. and Ratcliffe, M. (eds), *Improving Subject Teaching: Lessons from Research in Science Education*, 3–25, Routledge (Abingdon, Oxon).

Nelkin, D. (1995), *Selling Science: How the Press Covers Science and Technology*. W.H Freeman and Company (New York).

Osborne, J. (2000), Science for Citizenship, in Monk, M. and Osborne, J. (eds), *Good Practice in Science Teaching: What research has to say,* 225–240, Open University Press (Maidenhead).

Pearson, I. (2007), First Sir Gareth Roberts Science Policy Lecture, The Science Council, 6th November 2007, available at http://www.dius.gov.uk/speeches/pearson_sirgarethroberts_061107.html (accessed 23 May 2008).

Project 2061 (2008), Benchmarks Online, available at http://www.project2061.org/publications/bsl/online/index.php?chapter=1 (accessed 6 November 2008).

Rogers-Hayden, T. and Pidgeon, N. (2007), Moving Engagement 'Upstream'? Nanotechnologies and the Royal Society and Royal Academy of Engineering's Inquiry, *Public Understanding of Science* 16 (3), 345–364.

Rosser, S.V. (1997), *Re-Engineering Female Friendly Science.* Teachers College Press 9 New York).

Wynne, B. (1996), May the Sheep Safely Graze – A Reflexive View of the Expert-Lay Divide, in Lash, S. Szerszynski and Wynne, B. (eds), *Risk, Environment and Modernity,* 44–83, Sage (London).

Part II
Science Communication:
In Practice

Writing Science

Emma Weitkamp

4

Introduction

People learn about science from many different sources, but for most adults, once they leave formal education the media, in its broadest sense, is the main source of new information about science. In general terms, the media includes newspapers, magazines, books, radio, television, the Internet and other electronic media, and films. People learn about science through both fictional (e.g., novels and films) and non-fictional media (e.g., newspaper or magazine reports). For the purposes of this chapter, we will focus on non-fictional presentation of science and will further limit our discussion to written formats (e.g., newspapers, magazines and Internet).

The fact that most people rely on media sources for their information about science, rather than on scientists directly, places a responsibility on the science writer or journalist to report science accurately, clearly, fully and independently. Increasingly, reporters need to be aware not only of the science and technology themselves, but of their social and political contexts. These wider contexts may hide agendas that drive research or influence the interpretation of findings. It is not uncommon to hear reports in the media of organizations presenting results in a way that supports their particular cause, for example presenting environmental data so that it supports a particular course of action. The science writer needs to be aware of these wider motivations and view sources and information critically to avoid being misled.

> **LEARNING POINTS**
>
> *Theoretical learning points*
>
> - News values
> - News structure

Practical learning points

- News writing
- Feature writing
- Writing for the Internet
- Style for the science writer

Getting started

People are essentially story tellers and when science journalists talk about their writing they refer to 'the story'. But, what is a story? A story is something someone wants to hear or read. It needs to have a peg or angle, something you can use to grab the reader's attention, and it needs to have a purpose, a reason why the reader should read the story. Often, stories involve conflict, human interest, unusualness and importance. A good science writer will draw on his/her own interests, biases and strengths to develop a unique story. Bringing in the wider social, ethical and literary context can also lift a piece from the mundane to the exciting. These little 'extras' are what make the piece unique to you and worth a reader's attention.

There are six key principles or questions you will need to address to develop an interesting and appealing story:

1. Audience: Who are you writing for?
2. Purpose: Why are you writing this particular article? What do you hope to achieve?
3. Idea: Do you know what you want to say? Is it a good idea?
4. Information: Is information on your subject readily available?
5. Structure: Have you identified a story structure and does it match the content?
6. Contribution: Have you got something original to say about this topic?

Audience

Before you put pen to paper, develop a picture of your reader. What does (s)he look like? What does (s)he enjoy? Many writers have a mental picture of their reader. It might be their aunt, a neighbour or a friend. This mental picture is used to guide the content, structure and style of the piece by answering questions such as what would interest him or her about this story?

Science stories appear in almost all media, the trick is finding an angle that interests the readers. The same research findings might be reported in a special interest magazine (such as *Your Dog*), a women's magazine or a specialist science magazine, such as *New Scientist* or the BBC's *Focus* magazine, but the story will be quite different. The trick for the writer is to have a good understanding of who the audience is in order to make the story relevant and interesting. Researching the audience is just as important for stories written for the Internet as it is for other forms of popular science writing. Consider who uses the particular website for which you plan to write, how and why do they use that particular website? Answering these questions will help you develop a piece that people want to read and if the readers want to read it then the editor/publisher will want to run it.

You can learn a lot about the audience for a given publication simply by reading it, and in particular by examining the advertisements. This will give an indication of readers' interests, as well as socio-economic and educational background. Writing for a women's magazine is clearly different to writing for an electronics magazine, but a quick look at the news racks shows that there are vast differences within the women's magazine market alone. Understanding these differences is essential – editors only buy articles that fit their publication or website.

Purpose

The purpose is your reason for writing the article. Ask yourself: why am I interested in this topic? Why should other people be interested in the issue? You may have a specific purpose in mind; for example, you might feel strongly about an issue and want other people to share your views. In the fields of environment and health, the writer's purpose might be to change people's behaviour or to provide new information that will help them make better decisions about the environment or their health. In other areas, such as astronomy, you may simply want to share your interest and excitement about a subject with others. Knowing why you want to write about a particular aspect of science will help you develop an interesting idea for a story.

Idea

Good science writing offers something new to the reader: new information or just a new way of looking at well-known facts. It goes beyond a general subject area. A story on pheromones (body smells), for example, could be developed under a headline 'Nature nose best' giving a humorous twist to a story about the importance of smells.

Ideas tackle a specific aspect of a wider subject and often deal with problems, conflict, questions, drama or humour. Narrowing down the idea is a painstaking process. A story on biofuels, for example, could look at the potential for biofuels to cut carbon emissions and help meet Kyoto targets for reductions in greenhouse gas emissions or it could look at the potential impacts of biofuels on biodiversity. A little research using trusted Internet sites can help refine the ideas further turning up other research on the subject and even suggesting new avenues, such as new biofuel technologies.

Information

Identifying the available information is important in planning your article. It is no good pitching a 2000-word article to the editor and then finding you only have enough information to write a 500-word piece. Research will give you a good idea of how much information is available on your topic. The nature and complexity of the information available will give you an idea of the style and length of the article.

Structure

For printed media, two forms of science writing dominate: news and features. Both styles can be found in monthly magazines and in newspapers, but the structure, scope and intentions of the two formats are quite different. Both formats can also be found on the Internet, along with a variety of other writing styles ranging from formal essays to informal blogs. The Internet also offers many opportunities for interactivity which are not possible with more traditional print media. News, features and other Internet writing structures are discussed further in this chapter.

Contribution

What can you add to the story? Maybe you have particular insights or connections to the topic. If you surf or scuba dive, you might find an unusual angle for a story on marine biodiversity. If you're an amateur astronomer or ancient history buff, you might find an unusual approach to a story on a Mars probe. Perhaps you know someone working in a related field you could interview and who might offer fresh insights into the story.

Sources of science news and feature ideas

Ideas come from many sources, often at unexpected times and places. A handy notebook will keep you from losing these unexpected ideas, but there are also strategies you can use to find potential stories.

Science journalists, especially those working on newspapers, cover a wide range of science, often covering quantum physics one day and ecology the next. While they have a good idea of what makes an interesting story, they aren't experts in all fields of science. Add to this the often incremental and uncertain nature of scientific research and journalists are left with a difficult task: how to sift out the interesting and important new findings from yesterday's news or tomorrow's failed theory. Journalists develop their own preferred sources of stories. These may include:

- media releases, press conferences and press offices;
- science magazines, such as *The New Scientist*;
- peer-reviewed journals, such as *Science* and *Nature*;
- scientific conferences;
- research funders and organizations;
- personal contacts and tip offs

Many organizations now routinely send out news releases, from university press offices, to charities and non-governmental organizations as well as the commercial sector. A science journalist working for a daily newspaper might receive more than 25 media releases each day. Often written by professionals with a good understanding of the needs of journalists, media releases can offer interesting and easily accessible news stories. However, journalists wisely treat press releases with some scepticism as many promote a particular point of view or interpretation of data which may not be the only or even most commonly held view.

A number of websites now cater exclusively for science journalists (and press officers) offering a ready made source of media releases (try http://www.alphagalileo.org or http://www.eurekalert.org). Eurekalert also posts tip sheets (accessible only to registered journalists). These list the research papers which publishers have identified as being the most interesting articles to be published in forthcoming journal issues.

Fishing for stories directly from scientific journals is hard work but can yield original ideas. The difficulty is that the scientists writing for these journals aren't writing with you in mind; they are writing for other scientists. It isn't always obvious that an article titled 'Structural insights into mechanisms of catalysis and inhibition in Norwalk Virus polymerase' will lead to a story titled 'Scientists see Norwalk virus' Achilles heel' or that 'Selective Detection of Vapor Phase Hydrogen Peroxide with Phthalocyanine Chemiresistors' will turn into 'Sensors for homemade bombs'.

On the plus side, quality journals publishing original scientific research apply a system known as 'peer review'. Originally developed to ensure that the research studies published were of a high standard, the peer review system also provides journalists with some reassurance about the quality of the research and conclusions. The major interdisciplinary science journals run articles of broad interest to the scientific community and are a good place to look for interesting stories. These include *Nature, Science, The Proceedings of the National Academy of Science* and the PLOS journals (Public Library of Science, which hosts a series of open access journals where you can freely download the research papers). In the medical area, major interdisciplinary journals include *The New England Journal of Medicine, British Medical Journal* and *The Lancet*. Most scientific journals, however, are focused more narrowly on a scientific field and respected journals such as *Cell* are likely to publish some of the best research in their fields.

BOX 4.1   WHAT IS PEER REVIEW?

Peer review is a process that academic journals apply to research papers submitted for publication. The process involves sending research articles submitted for publication to researchers working in the same general field and asking for their comments and criticisms. This process of review by experts is designed to test whether the research and conclusions are sound and offers a measure of reassurance that research accepted for publication is credible.

The system is not without pitfalls. Some journals apply the peer review system more rigorously than others and even top notch journals do occasionally get it wrong.

ScienceDirect (sciencedirect.com) and PubMed (pubmedcentral.nih.gov/) provide searchable access to large numbers of scientific journals. Many publishers also now make their journals available online. Abstracts are usually available free, but most services charge for access to the full article.

Increasingly, science journals offer news services for journalists, with both *Science* and *Nature* providing media releases explaining key papers and making the original articles available to registered journalists on request. Media releases are sent to journalists in advance of the journal publication date under embargo (see Box 4.2). As a result, UK national newspapers, for example, are often full of science stories on Thursdays and Fridays when these journals are published.

BOX 4.2   EMBARGOES

An embargo is a notice not to publish information contained in a media release before a specified date and time. Organizations sometimes release information in advance to allow journalists time to prepare a news story, particularly when the information is highly technical or complex. The intention is to allow the journalist time to research and prepare a story. However, an embargo also prevents early publication, so in some senses it is a gag order.

Embargoes should be used with care. As the following excerpt provided by Toby Murcott (personal communication) illustrates:

A classic example of an embargo backfiring occurred on BBC Radio 4's morning news magazine programme, the influential *Today* programme. The Royal Society of Chemistry were about to publish a reasonably light-hearted piece of research on how to make the perfect cup of tea, a homage to an essay by George Orwell entitled

'The Eleven Steps to a Perfect Cup of Tea'. The Society had issued a press release and offered a key interviewee, which the *Today* programme picked up. They conducted a live interview in the programme. However, when the interviewer asked the researcher how to make the perfect cup of tea he replied that he was not allowed to say. It was being broadcast before the embargo. This had the effect of making both the researcher and the Royal Society of Chemistry look extremely foolish. If the opportunity arises to broadcast a story on a prestigious programme before an embargo time, take the opportunity and throw the embargo out of the window!

Scientific conferences and meetings offer an opportunity for stories about cutting-edge research and many of the bigger meetings have well-developed facilities for the media. Conferences offer the added benefit of being able to talk face to face with the scientists involved in the research, which can yield interesting story angles. However, budgetary constraints increasingly mean that science writers find it hard to justify attending all but the best-known meetings.

Research funders, such as the UK Research Councils (accessed through rcuk. ac.uk), CSIRO in Australia (csiro.au) and the European Commission (see for example, ec.europa.eu/research/index.cfm) all post information about funded research on their websites. In the United States, major government funded organizations, such as the National Aeronautics and Space Administration (nasa.gov) and the National Institutes of Health (nih.gov) are good sources of ideas and information.

Developing a portfolio of reliable contacts is also important for science writers. Although many science stories do not come directly from a 'tip off', reliable experts are invaluable for journalists investigating a potential story. Being able to ring up someone and ask for comment on a new piece of research not only saves time, it can quickly help identify stories which aren't based on good science.

Other sources of story ideas include announcements of research funding, prizes and other news media, including the online science newswire, sciencedaily.com.

All of these sources are good starting points but you should always investigate further. Tip sheets from journals are sometimes wrong and media releases, while helpful, can also be wrong or misleading. Always verify the information by referring to the original source, either the scientist involved or the original journal article. It is also worth double checking background information with other reliable sources.

Researching an idea

If using original research papers as a source or when researching an idea, it is worth developing a strategy to sift through the huge numbers of potentially

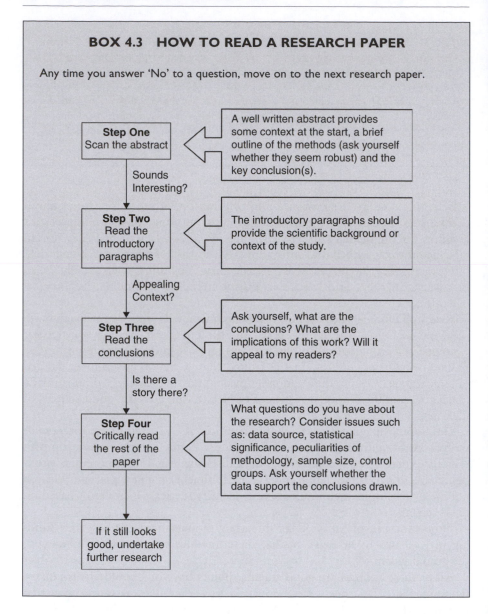

BOX 4.3   HOW TO READ A RESEARCH PAPER

Any time you answer 'No' to a question, move on to the next research paper.

Step One
Scan the abstract

A well written abstract provides some context at the start, a brief outline of the methods (ask yourself whether they seem robust) and the key conclusion(s).

Sounds Interesting?

Step Two
Read the introductory paragraphs

The introductory paragraphs should provide the scientific background or context of the study.

Appealing Context?

Step Three
Read the conclusions

Ask yourself, what are the conclusions? What are the implications of this work? Will it appeal to my readers?

Is there a story there?

Step Four
Critically read the rest of the paper

What questions do you have about the research? Consider issues such as: data source, statistical significance, peculiarities of methodology, sample size, control groups. Ask yourself whether the data support the conclusions drawn.

If it still looks good, undertake further research

interesting papers quickly. Scientific research papers use a style of academic writing which is quite different from the style used in popular science writing. A busy science writer hasn't got time to read through and digest in detail 10–15 research papers before deciding which one or two to research further. Fortunately, the process can be speeded up considerably by using the step by step approach outlined in Box 4.3. Found a good idea? Great! But don't start writing yet. Now it's time for research.

Find out what else has been published on the subject in scientific journals. You'll find some fields are very active with hundreds of reports each year, while others are not. If you are new to the field, then a general review article in a scientific journal will provide a broad context for the research. Even a Wikipedia entry can provide useful basic information on scientific terms.

Google the authors. University researchers often have research pages describing their current work and placing it in a broader scientific or social context. Finding out about the authors' research interests might suggest an unusual avenue for the story. Beware though that not all researchers update their pages as often as they should

Investigate other media reports on the topic. Knowing what has been published previously will help you identify a novel angle for your story; reading other media stories also tells you how other writers have approached the topic for their audiences.

Use an Internet search to find out the wider social context for the story. Are there other organizations with an interest in this field? In the case of healthcare stories, you may find patient groups online as well as businesses with an interest in the field. These may be useful sources to contact for comment on the research and their websites might suggest a personal or business angle for your story.

News writing

A hunt through any daily newspaper reveals a wide variety of science news. But why were these stories selected by science journalists over the hundreds if not thousands of research papers, reports and conference presentations published that day?

Science news, just like any other news, is what everyday people talk about and the skill of the science journalist is finding an angle on a new piece of research with wide appeal. A pretty tough job when you consider the abstract nature of much scientific research.

News by definition is something the reader doesn't already know – if they did, it wouldn't be new. In the case of science, finding a story that's new to the reader isn't difficult and it isn't enough either. With practice, journalists develop a 'nose' for news, an instinctive ability to identify newsworthy stories. Although finding news stories is a subjective process, research suggests that this 'nose for news' is built around a set of core news values (see Box 4.4). For further information on what makes news see Smith, 2007 or Harcup, 2004.

News values offer a guide to help identify interesting stories: those with significance, relevance, surprise, numbers or drama. But the ultimate question most journalists ask is: Does it interest me?

Finding a potential story is only the first step in constructing a news story. The key element is finding a 'peg' or 'hook' on which to hang the story. The 'peg' is the angle the writer takes in developing the story; it's what makes the story appealing to the reader and differentiates stories from different writers.

BOX 4.4   NEWS VALUES

Research shows that items generally fall into one or more of these categories to be considered news stories (Harcup and O'Neill 2001, 279). Although generated from a wide range of news, the categories can be applied to science.

Relevance
Stories that may have a direct impact on the reader (e.g., healthcare, environment, technology).

Surprise
Stories reporting unexpected findings.

Bad news (conflict stories)
Disasters, such as tidal waves, can be a peg for science stories, as can stories focusing on conflict between scientists.

Good news
New cures and treatments; technological advances are usually framed as good news.

Magnitude
Stories with a high potential impact or which might affect large numbers of people.

Entertainment
Interesting, fun facts and pretty science-based pictures all offer entertainment value.

Power Elite
Stories arising from research conducted at well-known institutions, by well-known scientists or published in top journals, such as *Science* and *Nature.*

Celebrity
Science stories sometimes focus on well-known people (scientists or other celebrities).

Follow ups
Stories already in the news that can be given a science twist.

Media agenda
Science stories that fit the organization's own agenda.

The following two extracts (Box 4.5) illustrate how different writers approach the same story about the creation of synthetic life. Bear in mind that the *New Scientist* is published weekly and this story appears nearly a week after the initial report. The author needs to find a unique angle and has also

BOX 4.5   APPROACHING A STORY

Pioneer's name written in synthetic DNA

Craig Venter has 'signed' his name into the sequence of the synthetic bacterial genome his lab created

Artists usually sign their work – and genomics pioneer Craig Venter is no exception. Written into the sequence of the synthetic bacterial genome unveiled last week is his name, his institute's, plus those of other key researchers involved.

The genome, modelled on the parasite *Mycoplasma genitalium* , is the longest stretch of synthetic DNA ever produced, at around 580,000 bases. 'We're pretty damned proud of what we've done, and we wanted to sign it,' says Venter. To make their marks, the team took the one-letter abbreviations for amino acids – 'C' for cysteine, 'R' for arginine, 'A' for alanine, and so on – and included the corresponding DNA sequences in their synthetic genome (*Science*, DOI: 10.1126/science.1151721).

These 'watermarks' also have a serious purpose. The plan is to transplant the synthetic genome into a living *Mycoplasma* cell, in the hope that it will 'boot up'. The watermark sequences will provide a good way of verifying if the transplant is successful by allowing researchers to distinguish between artificial and natural DNA. Venter adds that the watermarks will also help protect the group's intellectual property, making it harder for others to use the synthetic genome without permission.

Drew Endy, a bioengineer at the Massachusetts Institute of Technology, agrees that [they] should 'barcode' their products. This would allow for the rapid detection of synthetic DNA, which may ease growing concerns over the risks of escaping into the environment. It could also provide an identity tag with information about a sequence.

But Endy urges synthetic biologists to agree on a standardized watermark system, and to research methods that will ensure that such 'barcode' sequences do not cause unpredictable biological effects.

Source: New Scientist, 2 February 2008.

Playing god: The man who would create artificial life

The possibility of a synthetic life form created in a laboratory has come tantalizingly close to reality after scientists announced yesterday that they have generated the largest man-made molecule of DNA – the chemical blueprint of life.

For the first time researchers, led by the controversial American scientific entrepreneur Craig Venter, have manufactured the entire DNA genome of a free-living micro-organism. This means that 'artificial life' is on the verge of being created in a test tube.

The huge DNA molecule represents the single chromosome that makes up the complete genome of Mycoplasma genitalium, a parasitic microbe that lives in the reproductive tract. Dr Venter and his colleagues made the chromosome from scratch by placing each of its 582,970 individual chemical units in their correct genetic sequence.

> The monumental achievement was the final step necessary before the scientists attempt their ultimate goal of inserting the synthetic genome into the empty 'shell' of a non-living cell to see if they can create a fully replicating, man-made organism....
>
> Dr Venter brushed aside questions about the ethics of creating artificial life forms, saying that there have been extensive discussions and debates on the issue long before the research began in earnest some years ago.
>
> In his recent autobiography, Dr Venter holds out the promise of a new type of micro-factory or laboratory of the future based on synthetic life forms created as a result of the work on *Mycoplasma genitalium*, which he suggests may be renamed *Mycoplasma laboratorium*.
>
> 'If our plan succeeds, a new creature will have entered the world, albeit one that relies on an existing organism's cellular machinery to read its artificial DNA', Dr Venter says.
>
> 'We have often been asked if this will be a step too far. I always reply that – so far at least – we are only reconstructing a diminished version of what is already out there in nature.'
>
> *Source:* Connor, S., *The Independent,* 25 January 2008, p. 4.

had some time to delve into the story. In contrast, the news report published in *The Independent*, a UK daily newspaper, was published on the same day that the research article appeared in *Science*. It takes a hard news approach of giving the facts of the development, but also raises questions about the ethics associated with this type of research.

News structures

News is about telling a story but not in the conventional format of beginning, middle and end. Save that style for non-news material and instead start a news story at the end. For science news, that usually means putting the researcher's main findings right at the start and then explaining why those findings are important. This 'blurt it out and explain' structure has become known as the inverted pyramid (see Box 4.6).

News stories start with the most important or hard hitting information. This is the information you want all readers to understand and can be thought of as the 'story in a nutshell'. Then build your story by elaborating and explaining the key point made in the first paragraph. This inverted structure serves two purposes:

- it meets the needs of readers who can read as much or as little of the story as they want without missing your main point (and only a few will make it all the way to the end).
- it allows the subeditor to cut the bottom of the story if space is tight without chopping off key points or the conclusions.

BOX 4.6   THE INVERTED PYRAMID

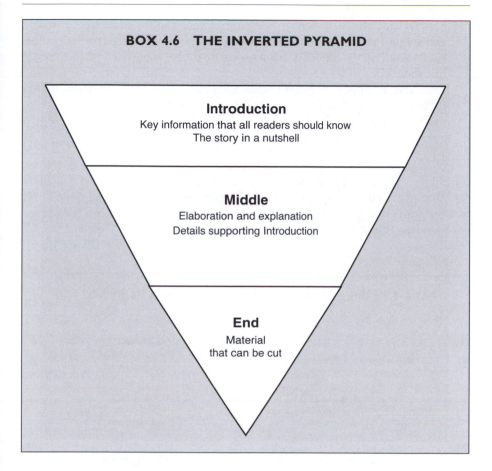

Introduction
Key information that all readers should know
The story in a nutshell

Middle
Elaboration and explanation
Details supporting Introduction

End
Material
that can be cut

News stories should answer a set of key questions, commonly known as the 5 Ws and H: 'Who?', 'What?', 'Where?', 'When?', 'Why?' and 'How?' You can think of these questions as the questions the reader wants answered:

- What is interesting about this piece of science? – this is the main news hook.
- Why is it interesting? – this question seeks to make the finding relevant to the reader, explaining why the reader should be interested in this new finding.
- Who made the discovery? – this is the researcher's name and is often provided as part of a quote.
- Where did it happen? – the place where the research was carried out, for example the name of a university.
- When did it happen? – for news by definition this is recently. However, bear in mind the different publication timescales for a newspaper (daily), magazines (weekly, monthly or even quarterly) and the Internet (could be

hourly) and you will start to see that 'when' can be addressed in many ways. For a newspaper, the when might be 'reported at a scientific conference yesterday', while for a magazine it might be 'reported at a conference this month'.

■ How did it happen? – not all science stories answer this question. When they do, they tend to focus on the obstacles that were overcome to make the break through or a brief report of the methods the scientists used to generate their findings.

Following the inverted pyramid structure suggests that these questions should be answered near the start of the story. For science stories, it is usually the 'What' and 'Why' questions that need to be answered first and the 'Who', 'Where' and 'When' can be placed lower down the article to keep the reader engaged (see Box 4.7).

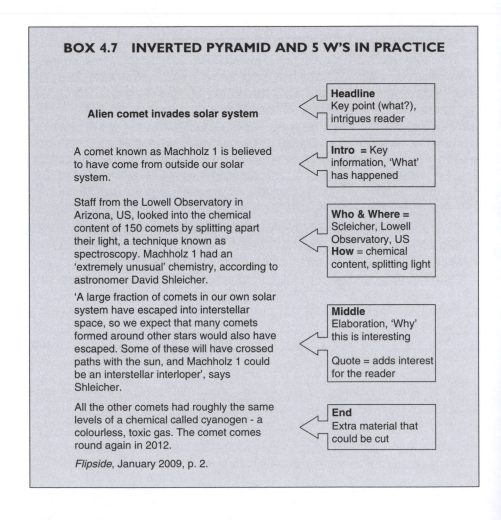

BOX 4.7   INVERTED PYRAMID AND 5 W'S IN PRACTICE

Alien comet invades solar system

> **Headline**
> Key point (what?), intrigues reader

A comet known as Machholz 1 is believed to have come from outside our solar system.

> **Intro** = Key information, 'What' has happened

Staff from the Lowell Observatory in Arizona, US, looked into the chemical content of 150 comets by splitting apart their light, a technique known as spectroscopy. Machholz 1 had an 'extremely unusual' chemistry, according to astronomer David Shleicher.

> **Who & Where =** Scleicher, Lowell Observatory, US
> **How** = chemical content, splitting light

'A large fraction of comets in our own solar system have escaped into interstellar space, so we expect that many comets formed around other stars would also have escaped. Some of these will have crossed paths with the sun, and Machholz 1 could be an interstellar interloper', says Shleicher.

> **Middle**
> Elaboration, 'Why' this is interesting
>
> Quote = adds interest for the reader

All the other comets had roughly the same levels of a chemical called cyanogen - a colourless, toxic gas. The comet comes round again in 2012.

> **End**
> Extra material that could be cut

Flipside, January 2009, p. 2.

Headlines – a reader's first taste of the story

News stories don't have titles they have headlines. On newspapers, these key reader grabbers are not actually written by the science writer, but rather by the subeditor or 'sub' for short. The sub's job is to layout the page, deciding how to organize the stories on the page. Whether a story runs down one column or across two has a big impact on the length of the headline. That's why subs write them. Even if it isn't the headline that actually appears in the story, working up a possible headline helps you focus your ideas and get to the heart of the story.

There is a great skill in writing successful headlines, where every letter counts in the writer's bid to get across the story in a small space. Zealously focusing on the tight space available can lead to some funny results, if the writer doesn't step back and consider the final version. Consider these examples:

Panda Mating Fails: Veterinarian Takes Over
Lung Cancer in Women Mushrooms
Plane Too Close To Ground, Crash Probe Told
Two Soviet Ships Collide, One Dies
Miners Refuse To Work After Death

The introduction – your most important paragraph

Getting the introduction right is crucially important. It sets the tone for the article and provides an essential hook by which to capture your readers. The secret of a well-written introduction for a news piece is to keep it short and to the point, often with a maximum of 20 words, comprising one or two sentences.

Consider the following examples:

Without a single living specimen to observe, how do you figure out how an extinct species moved? Penn State palaeontologist Alan Walker and his team found a clue to mammals' motion in an unlikely place: their ears. (*Discover*, October 2007, p. 16)

The prospect of finding life elsewhere in the universe has been boosted by the discovery of carbon-based molecules in the atmosphere of a planet outside our solar system. (*Sydney Morning Herald*, 21 March 2008, p. 13)

In the first example, the author starts by posing a scientific question, but using easily accessible language. The reader's interest is then piqued by using language suggestive of investigation ('clue') and surprise ('in an unlikely place'). In the second example the writer draws on a general interest in finding life elsewhere in the universe: effectively the 'are we alone?' question. Both stories start by telling you an essential bit of new information (that ears can help us understand mammalian movement, and that organic molecules have been found on a planet outside our solar system). The intention is that these small nuggets of information leave you wanting to know more and stimulate you to read on. However, even if you've lost interest, you've learned a new fact.

Winning science features

Unlike news, feature styles vary a great deal. However, as with fictional stories, science features always come in three parts: a beginning (introduction), middle (also called the body text) and an end.

Introductions

Many writers consider the introduction the most important part of the story; it is used to grab the reader's attention and pique their curiosity. Without a good introduction, a story has no readers. Think about the lead as seduction – use the introduction to pull the reader in.

BOX 4.8   GRABBING ATTENTION

The introduction needs to make the reader want to read on. Five successful opening styles are illustrated below:

▪ **The bold statement:** Using a strong statement forces readers to sit up and take notice. They either have to agree with what you have said or disagree. Either way, you've got their attention and, hopefully, jogged them enough to persuade them to read on.

If you allow a chicken to live like a chicken, eat like a chicken and behave like a chicken, it will end up tasting like a chicken ought to taste – delicious.

Source: Hugh Fearnley-Whittingstall (2008), 'The changing face of food', *Country Living*, April, p. 84.

▪ **General statements:** Marshal your facts and make a broad sweeping statement – even better if it is one that not everyone agrees with – then focus in on some key facts. This type of opening is challenging though, as general statements can seem trite or lead to a 'so what, we all know that' response from readers.

Almost all scientists now agree that the climate changes we are seeing are due to human activity, especially the burning of fossil fuels such as oil, gas and coal. Current predictions are for a temperature rise of at lest 1.5–2°C by 2100. To put that in context, the average temperature difference between Plymouth and Edinburgh is between 1°C and 2°C. And if we don't change our behaviour radically, the change could be 6°C. Along with the warming comes a sea-level rise of at least 50 cm (18 inches), but potentially as much as 2 m (over 6 feet).

Source: Brian Eversham (2007), 'Adapting to climate change', *Natural World*, Winter, p. 18.

▪ **Raise a question:** Questions can be used to get the reader thinking about your topic. It is a direct way to engage the reader and make them want to know more.

It used to be so easy. Getting your parents out of bed at 6am, armed with something loud was the only way to start the day. Now it's all too much like hard work getting up any time before 10am. How come mornings suddenly turned out to be only good for sleeping?

Source: Chris Edwards (2006), 'Wakey Wakey', *Flipside*, November, p. 14.

■ **Descriptive openings:** Use visual language to paint a picture in the reader's mind and engage the reader with your topic.

At 9:00 in the evening on January 29, just as President George W. Bush was about to begin his first State of the Union address, I gathered with three anxious scientists in a small, windowless laboratory in Worcester, Massachusetts. We were at Advanced Cell Technology – a privately owned biotechnology company that briefly made international headlines last fall by publishing the first scientific account of cloned human embryos. The significance of the achievement was debatable: the company's most successful embryo had reached only six cells before it stopped dividing (one other had reached four cells, another had reached two) – a fact that led to a widespread dismissal, in the media and the scientific community, of ACT's 'breakthrough'. The work was largely judged to be preliminary, inconsequential, and certainly not worthy of headlines. Many people in political and religious circles, however, had a decidedly different view. They deemed ACT's work an ethical transgression of the highest order and professed shock, indignation, and horror.

Source: 'Cloning Trevor', *Atlantic Monthly*, June 2002.

■ **Intriguing openings:** Sometimes writers use openings that don't immediately indicate what the story is about. This leaves the reader wondering what's going on and wanting to know more.

A 29-year-old paralegal was lying in the middle of Congress Street in downtown Boston after being run over by a bicycle messenger, and her first thought was whether her skirt was hiking up. 'Oh, why did I wear a skirt today?' she asked herself. 'Are these people all looking at my underpants?'

Her second thought was whether she would be hit by one of the cars speeding down Congress – she wasn't aware that other pedestrians had gathered around, some of them directing traffic away from her. And her third thought was of a different trauma, eight years earlier, when driving home one night, she was sitting at a red light and found herself confronted by an armed drug addict, who forced his way into her car, made her drive to an abandoned building and tried to rape her.

'I had a feeling that this one trauma, even though it was a smaller thing, would touch off all sorts of memories about the time I was carjacked,' said the woman, whose name is Kathleen. She worried because getting over that carjacking was something that had taken Kathleen a long time. 'For eight months at least,' she said, 'every night before I went to bed, I'd think about it. I wouldn't be able to sleep, so I'd get up and make myself a cup of decaf tea, watch something on TV to get myself out of that mood. And every morning I'd wake up feeling like I had a gun against my head.'

Source: 'The Quest to Forget', *The New York Times*, 4 April 2004.

Body text

The workhorse of the story, body text is where you make your key points. Here you should marshal facts and reveal their significance. Structures vary depending on the nature of the subject, preference of the writer and perceived interests of the reader but it must hang together logically. As the story unfolds, consider what questions your readers might have and answer these as you go along. But, beware of the aimless meandering stroll around the subject.

Features combine some or all of the following elements: facts, quotes, description, analysis, opinions and anecdotes. Facts are essential in science writing and these will need to be researched and double checked. Direct quotes add authority and interest to the piece and are a good way to bring in controversy. Description helps readers understand the concept and bring the story alive. Along with metaphors and analogies, well-written description can help the reader's understanding as well as engaging them with the story.

Use analysis to help the reader understand the wider social and political contexts surrounding science stories. This can be particularly important in stories covering controversial topics, such as stem cells or responses to climate change. Opinion also has its role to play in some types of science features. While many stories stick to the facts, opinion can be brought in when discussing the wider social context surrounding scientific research. Used with care, anecdotes can add a personal touch, humanizing a story which might otherwise seem abstract.

Endings

Features have more rounded endings than news stories, which often end with the least important information. Typically, endings to feature stories tie off any loose ends or return to points raised in the introduction. They can also introduce new twists, leaving the reader to ponder unanswered questions.

Structural issues

A logical structure is at the core of good science writing, whether it is a feature piece or news item. The story must start at the beginning and end at the end. But even in the middle, paragraphs need to be lined up in a logical order and the sentences need to build one upon the other. Consider the sentences below. Which seems more logical?

> Experts suggest reduced protein content in major foods could have consequences for human nutrition. New analysis suggests that rising CO_2 levels will affect the protein content of major food crops, and indeed this may already be taking place. Nitrogen-based fertilizers have a high environmental cost, but farmers can use them to limit the effects of rising CO_2 levels.

> New analysis suggests that rising CO_2 levels will affect the protein content of major food crops, and indeed this may already be taking place. Experts suggest this change in composition of the foods we eat could have consequences for human nutrition. Farmers can limit these effects by using more nitrogen-based fertilizers, but these in turn have a high environmental cost.

Ann Finkbeiner suggests a good rule of thumb, 'begin each sentence with the word or phrase that ended the previous sentence'. She illustrates this point: '"Because the speed of light is constant, we see galaxies that are distant in space also distant in time." That sentence is grammatically respectable and factually accurate, but for the lay reader, it's close to nonsense.' She goes on to transform that sentence using her logic rule 'The only way we see galaxies is by their light. Light leaving a galaxy at a certain distance and travelling a fixed speed takes, say 100 years before we see it. We see the image of the galaxy as it was 100 years ago'(cited in Blum et al. 2006). Finkbeiner argues that this AB/BC/CD approach also works on the paragraph level as a way of making transitions between paragraphs.

Transition sentences can be used as a way of making connections between ideas. They make a link between two ideas, explaining why having just read something you should move on to read the next idea. Transition words can be as simple as 'and' or 'but', though variety is important. Linking words could be:

As long as
Note
That includes
Though
Also
This prompted
It was
It turns out
As we have seen
Again
A bigger surprise
Surprisingly
Unusually

Explaining science

As well as explaining what something is, it can be helpful to explain what it is not. Giving non-examples helps the reader understand what lies both within and without the subject boundaries.

Style for the science writer

Good style focuses on short simple sentences with few clauses. Known as the KISS (keep it short and simple) principle, the average length of a punchy sentence is less than 20 words. Sentence structure should be kept simple, with no more than one subsidiary clause. Using short simple sentences also makes it easier to use correct grammar and punctuation. Information overload and lots of punctuation make it hard for the reader to follow the story.

Limit paragraphs to one idea. Once you've finished with that thought, move on to the next paragraph, even if you have only written one sentence. A quick check in any newspaper will soon show that the once unbreakable rule that a paragraph should have at least three sentences is routinely broken in news rooms across the world.

Put the most important word at the end of the sentence and the most important sentence at the end of the paragraph. You remember best what you heard last.

BOX 4.9   FOG INDEX

The Fog Index is a typical measure of the complexity of your writing. To calculate the Fog Index, take an extract of 100 words that finishes at the end of a sentence. Divide this by the number of sentences to get your average sentence length. Then count up the number of words with three or more syllables, leaving out capitalized words and verbs with prefixes or suffixes. Add this number to the average sentence length and then multiply by 0.4. This is your Fog Index. A Fog Index of 10 is the level of an average 15-year old secondary school pupil. A Fog Index of over 18 is the upper limit of complexity used by broad sheet newspapers. You can get a feel for whether your writing is at a suitable level for the publication by calculating the Fog Index for the publication and comparing it with your writing.

Attribution, or quotes, lift a story and give authority to the points you are making. Most news and feature stories include quotes from the scientists involved in the study and longer stories will normally include quotes from other scientists or people with an interest in the subject. Direct quotes, marked out in quotation marks, can bring a story to life, giving insight into the importance of the subject and its relevance to the reader.

Pace

Keeping readers hooked right to the end of the story is partly about setting a good pace. Pace should vary, sometimes quick or building anticipation and at other times slower with more description. In either case, a reader who is reading quickly is more likely to reach the final paragraph than one who is bogged down in the detail or re-reading complex sentences in order to understand them.

A fast paced story uses active, powerful verbs. Avoid passive sentence constructions, they can almost always be rewritten using active verbs. Vary your sentence length. Short sharp sentences speed up the pace, but too many make a paragraph seem choppy. Play with alliteration and sentence structures that create rhythms.

Traditionally, news is told in the past tense, because news reports something that has already happened. Feature stories are often told in the present to create a sense of immediacy or adventure.

BOX 4.10   ACTIVE VERSUS PASSIVE SENTENCES

	Active sentence construction	*Passive sentence construction*
Definition	When the subject of the sentence performs the action of the verb	The subject of the sentence receives the action of the verb
Examples	▪ Scientists found a new planet. ▪ Plants absorb CO_2. ▪ Heat, trapped in the earth's atmosphere by CO_2, is a major contributor to climate change.	▪ A new planet was found by scientists. ▪ CO_2 is absorbed by plants. ▪ Climate change is caused by heat trapped in the earth's atmosphere by CO_2.

Analogies, clichés and jargon – dos and don'ts

Help the reader by using analogies and metaphors to explain complex scientific concepts. Metaphors can be explanatory or emotional and both can add considerably to the reader's understanding. Explanatory metaphors help the reader to understand new concepts by relating them to existing knowledge. Emotional metaphors influence the feel of a piece and help put across the writer's beliefs, particularly in comment pieces. Use metaphor carefully and sparingly, avoiding mixed metaphors (applying two metaphors to a concept at the same time).

Analogies also help make science vivid and engaging, but don't over use them and avoid clichés like the plague. Get in the habit of jargon-busting. There is no easier way to lose a reader than to bring in jargon and scientific language.

Balance

A well-written story should be balanced. This means exploring the research findings from a number of different points of view. For some stories, the research findings will be controversial or point to different courses of action. Here, balance involves explaining these different views. For example, research on genetically modified crops is seen by some scientists as offering the next green revolution and a potential solution to world hunger, while other scientists raise concerns about the potential environmental harm such crops might cause.

For other stories, the findings may not be contested, but exploring the views of different people or groups who may be affected by the findings will lift the story, adding interest. For example, a new effective treatment for a serious disease, such as heart disease, is likely to be viewed positively by both doctors and patients, but a patient could give a much more personal insight into the potential benefits.

Balance adds credibility to the story and can be used to help the reader understand the issues at stake. Importantly, balance adds interest for the reader and draws them deeper into the article.

Accuracy versus caveats

Accuracy is also important. An inaccurate news item might as well be fiction. Beware, a journalist's notion of accuracy is not the same as a scientist's. With science news, there is a balance to be struck between accurately reporting the new findings and including the caveats and uncertainties that crowd scientific reports and interviews. For the science writer, the trick is to report what the findings show while leaving out some of the finer nuances or uncertainties associated with the research. It is not an easy balance to be struck, as most scientists hedge their findings with statements such as:

There is an 85 per cent probability that...
Under optimal conditions we achieved...

If in doubt, check your understanding with the researchers. Few journalists will send draft stories to researchers for approval, but it is normal practice to ring them up to discuss the story. At the same time as fishing for good quotes or a better angle, you can check that you have understood the story correctly and if you are still uncertain when you've written your first draft, there is nothing wrong with calling them again to double check the facts.

And finally: edit, edit, edit

Be a word miser and make your points as economically as possible. Ask yourself 'is this sentence, thought or point crucial to the story?' If the answer is no, then take it out. Good writing is sharp and to the point, so explore ways to express your ideas clearly and concisely.

Take a hard look at words such as 'there' and 'it' and only rarely should 'the' or 'very' appear in a story. Consider, 'the moon shone very brightly' versus 'the moon shone brightly'. A story full of adverbs will appear all puff and no substance, so sprinkle them in lightly.

Writing for the Internet

Recent developments in web technology mean that it is now even easier to get your ideas online. This so called 'user generated content' can take many forms, whether it is through contributions to discussion groups, via sites designed to collect new content from the audience and redistribute it or through blogs. Using a model coined 'Citizen Journalism' or 'Participatory Journalism' these sites break down the traditional barriers between the writer or contributor and the audience, with many contributors also forming part of the audience (see Bowman and Willis 2003).

Essentially, Citizen Journalism refers to non-professional writers gathering and disseminating new information. In effect, these non-professional writers act as journalists, contributing to the flow of news and information into the public sphere. But unlike professional journalists who are paid to find interesting new information, anyone can contribute to many online discussion fora and other types of websites, albeit usually without payment.

Whether you are seeking to contribute to a website as a professional (paid) journalist or in a citizen capacity, you should approach to opportunity professionally. Just as with print media, you should research the site. What opportunities does it provide? Do they take news? Features?

You might also consider setting up your own blog (see for example http://boingboing.net), which will allow a more personal, informal style. Whichever approach you take, remember that writing for the Internet follows the same principles of good writing as news and feature stories. There are some differences though.

Nature of the audience

Two main issues arise in relation to Internet audiences: narrowcasting and searching behaviours. Many Internet sites are designed to cater for specific groups, often quite tightly defined. While a newspaper has a specific audience in mind, it is likely to be less narrowly defined than that of many niche Internet sites.

Another issue to consider is that Internet users are often looking (searching) for specific information. A reader pulling up your story on the Internet may already be interested in the subject, compared with a newspaper reader who comes across science articles within a rich mix of politics and social commentary. Thinking about how the reader might find your story could help shape the story. This, of course, is not true of all readers or all Internet sites, many of which (such as the BBC or the websites of publishing companies) provide a context which is more like print media.

Screen size

Advice on writing for the web often focuses on the need for short articles that fill one or two screens and little more. Few people like to scroll through huge long chunks of text, so finding ways to keep the article short but providing more depth at the click of the mouse is an option worth exploring. Sites vary though and ultimately the length of the piece will be determined by the Internet site itself.

Interactivity

One of the great advantages of the Internet is the potential for interactivity and to offer more than the static text and pictures of print media. Even if you aren't a programmer, you can suggest flash animations to accompany your story, provide ideas for quizzes, invite reader comment or even suggest a vote on a controversial topic (for examples, see http://firstscience.com). Other ideas include incorporating picture galleries, forums and blogs.

Link out

If there are other good sources of information on the topic, suggest hyperlinks. These can be problematic from the host's perspective as they allow readers an opportunity to escape from the website, but for the reader wanting more in-depth information these are highly valuable.

Writing blogs

While many of the principles of good style, such as short, clear sentences and avoiding jargon, should be considered, blogs break many of the rules of good style outlined in this chapter.

Blogs take many styles and formats, from breaking news through to personal diary or miniessays. Most are informal or less formal in style than, say a newspaper.

Whether news or commentary, blog entries are usually presented in reverse chronological order (i.e., newest entries at the top). Their informal style means that they do not conform to a specific structure. Length also varies tremendously from short snippets of information to longer, more considered commentary.

Several genre of blogs already exist, such as:

- **Personal blogs:** still the most common, personal blogs are a diary or commentary by one individual (see for example: http://www.monbiot.com/)
- **Corporate blogs:** are run by a company or organization and may be public (as in this University blog: http://difference.weblog.glam.ac.uk/) or private (restricted to company employees)
- **Group written blogs:** blogs can be written by more than one person, spreading out the work of providing regular entries (see for example: http://scienceblogs.com/)
- **Q &A:** some blogs are developed in response to questions from readers with the blogger providing answers (see for example: http://www.cbc.ca/health/health-blog/2008/01/ask_an_expert.html).

As more writers turn to blogging, it is certain that other blog genre will soon emerge. However, one point is important, for a blog to be effective it needs to be maintained and updated regularly. Who wants to return to a blog even one week later to find no new entries?

Conclusion

Breaking into mainstream journalism is justifiably challenging, but with the advent of the Internet the boundaries between professional journalists and citizen journalists are blurring. For the science writer, whether a professional writer or scientist, there is a wide range of outlets for good quality, well-thought out and carefully crafted writing. For the student of science writing the timing couldn't be better.

ACTIVITIES

- What types of science do you find interesting and why? Cataloguing your interests in science will help you identify which areas you are most comfortable writing about. Thinking about the 'why' question will help you develop angles which you could pursue. Write a 300–500 word 'blog' about your interests in science.
- Keep a journal or scrapbook. Write down interesting ideas you come across about science. This is good practice from a writing perspective and it will help you develop your science ideas. Collect clippings of stories you enjoyed in a scrapbook. Write down why you liked each story.
- Take a piece you have written and cut it down by 20 per cent.

References and further reading

Blum, D., Knudson, M., Henig, R.M. (eds) (2006), *A field guide for science writers, The official guide of the National Association of Science writers*, 2nd Ed, Oxford University Press (Oxford).

Bowman, S. and Willis, C. (2003), We Media: How audiences are shaping the future of news and information. Available online from http://www.hypergene.net/wemedia/weblog.php

Freedman, S.M., Dunwoody, S. and Rogers, C.L. (1999) *Communicating Uncertainty: Media Coverage of New and Controversial Science*, Lawrence Erlbaum Associates (Mahwah, NJ).

Harcup, T. (2004), *Journalism Principles and Practice*, Sage (London).

Hennessy, B. (1997), *Writing Feature Articles*, 3rd edn, Focal Press (London).

Harcup, T. and O'Neill, D. (2001), What is News? Galtung and Ruge Revisited, *Journalism Studies*, 2 (2), 261–280.

Hicks, W. (1998), *English for Jjournalists*, 2nd edn, Routledge (London).

Smith, J. (2007), *Essential Reporting, the NCTJ Guide for Trainee Journalists*, Sage (London).
Weitkamp, E.L.C. (2003), British Newspapers Privilege Health and Medicine Topics over Other Science News, *Public Relations Review*, 29 (3): 321–333.

Useful websites

Associations for Science Writers

Association of British Science Writers: http://www.absw.org.uk
National Association of Science Writers (US): http://www.nasw.org
European science journalists associations: http://www.esf.org/eusja/
Australian Science Communicators: http://www.asc.asn.au/

News sources

Alphagalileo, a European science press release service: http://www.alphagalileo.org
Eurekalert, a press release service run by the American Association for the Advancement of Science: http://www.eurekalert.org

Broadcasting Science

Toby Murcott

5

This chapter explores science broadcasting from the perspectives of both scientists and science communicators seeking coverage of science and of potential science journalists, producers or presenters. This chapter covers pitching ideas for radio/TV, scripting, interviewing, producing and editing. It will also provide a brief guide to the different roles in TV and radio production and an outline of the different types of programmes. It is a practical chapter designed to introduce the complex and exciting world of science broadcasting.

LEARNING POINTS

Theoretical learning points

- The intimate link between the development of broadcasting and the development of technology.
- Strict regulations governing the use of broadcasting technology.

Practical learning points

- Broadcast genre
- How to get your story to air
- Roles in broadcasting

A century of broadcasting

The history of broadcast media is an interlinked mix of uneven developments in the technology of transmission and reception, commercial interests, regulation and the role of governments, as well as the interruptions but also opportunities of major national and international events. The unevenness of developments is readily illustrated. Neville Chamberlain, the British Prime Minister's return from meeting with Hitler in Munich in 1938 was broadcast live on radio *and* television (Richard Dimbleby's commentary on the event was carried by both media). But even radio would have been of little use in those rural communities of 1930s Finland or the United States which did not yet have an electricity supply. Yet it was only around a decade later, in 1949, that the moon was televised for the first time, through a telescope. And what Queen Elizabeth II's 1953 Coronation famously did for the spread of television in Britain, her post-Coronation tour of the Commonwealth did for radio in New Zealand (Day 1994, p. 312). While just nine years later, in 1962, 'space age' technology meant Telstar I inaugurated satellite relays of American television programmes.

Almost from the beginning, broadcasting is a worldwide phenomenon. And everywhere, the development of radio was accompanied by fears that print media would suffer as a result, much as the later development of TV was accompanied by fears that radio would suffer in its turn. Will TV and radio suffer with the development of new media in the twenty-first century? Or will the former continue to exploit the latter – in the way that the press, radio and television have all made a place for themselves via the Internet?

The year 1922 is a major landmark. Between January and July 1922, 430 new radio stations had been licensed by the US Department of Commerce, (15 times the number licensed in 1921) (Barnouw 1966, p. 91). Marconi's London station 2LO opened with the first broadcast of a boxing commentary in May 1922, followed in October by the creation of the British Broadcasting Company, formed, among others, by six leading radio manufacturers. The broadcast receiving licence was introduced at £10/- (50p), half of which went to the BBC which also benefited from royalties on radio equipment sold. The first daily transmissions from 2LO started in November, and in December, John C. W. Reith was appointed General Manager of the Company, aged only 33. By the end of 1922, 35,774 licenses had been issued, the British Broadcasting Company Ltd had formally been registered and boasted a staff of four. Even in so small a country as New Zealand (with a population of not much over a million at the time) there were seven radio stations by the end of 1922.

These early beginnings also illuminate the critical distinction between commercial and public service broadcasting. Though the British Broadcasting Company Ltd began as a monopoly it was also a commercial company. The granting of a Royal Charter in 1927, however, marked its transformation into the British Broadcasting Corporation (BBC) a state-owned monopoly, with John Reith (later Lord Reith) as its first director-general. His vision of the value and power of broadcasting imbued the entire BBC output until the 1950s and 60s. He was wholly committed to ensuring that every programme was educational or informative, with the aim of achieving higher cultural standards for all. As a result, he adopted a policy of mixed programming.

This involved retaining just a single channel on which all kinds of provision – religion, classical and light music, news, sports etc. – was carried, hoping that listeners would not switch off, but, 'keeping the radio on be exposed to content of which they had little prior knowledge and thus be educated – achieving the Reithian 'cultural uplift' (Pegg 1983, p. 207).

The BBC and Reith's example of public service broadcasting has long served as the model for the organization of broadcasting across the world – with the major exception of the United States. Reith's vision entailed 'an active faith that a supply of good things will create a demand for them, not waiting for the demand to express itself' (quoted in Barnouw 1966, p. 248). American thinking appeared to turn this on its head: public taste was to be catered for, courted and competed for by the commercial provision of broadcasting. As a prominent historian of broadcasting in America put it: 'To the men of the BBC the chaos of American radio (in the 1930s) seemed an extraordinary phenomenon. ... The eruption of competing networks, vying for public events as well as advertising dollars, created a bizarre picture, totally unlike the more orderly BBC' (Barnouw 1966, p. 248).

It was into this world of radio contrasts that experiments with television were launched. The first BBC transmission of 30 line experimental television took place in 1929 (by which date the BBC's staff had grown to 1,109), while RCA (Radio Corporation of America) demonstrated it at New York World's Fair in 1939. The Second World War interrupted progress: in both the United States and Britain, transmission ceased and did not resume until after its end in 1945. A year later, however, televisions went on sale in the United States, and CBS (Columbia Broadcasting Service) and NBC (National Broadcasting Company) were demonstrating colour.

Radio was similarly altered during the war, but, it was not just wartime conditions that meant a radical change in its role but the post-war rise of television. Radio developed in different directions as if filling in gaps television could not provide. For example, 1944 saw the rise of disk-jockeying in America. On both sides of the Atlantic there was a proliferation of commercial and later specialist radio stations, including local radio, black or minority stations and developments such as citizen band radio (from the 1960s). Radio Caroline's first pirate radio transmission from a ship anchored off the Essex coast was in 1964, the same year that the BBC's staff numbered 10,836 and that *Match of the Day* and, in this context, most notably the flagship science programme, *Horizon* were first televised.

Tuning in to science

You can hear or see science in many different places across the airwaves. Some are obvious, such as dedicated science programmes, some less so, such as drama or even comedy routines. The focus of most science communicators is on the places most likely to broadcast science, the dedicated science programmes and the news. However, it is important to recognize that science can and does appear anywhere. You should always think broadly and creatively about how you might get your message on air.

Science broadcasting is now seen as a specific genre, produced on the whole by specialist teams and with a wide but specific brief. It tends to feature more on public service than commercial broadcasters and pure science is very hard to find on commercial radio stations. It is important to recognize that science, like any other genre, is not broadcast to educate an audience about science, but to attract a specific audience in competition with other media. As a result current science programmes reflect the general trends in the wider media.

BOX 5.1   CASE STUDY: BBC *HORIZON*

Horizon is the BBC TV flagship science programme. It has tackled complex and difficult science during its 44 years on air, such as the discovery of HIV, the solution of Fermat's Last Theorem and a seminal programme on the rise of the silicon chip. More recently, though, it has been criticized for focusing more on human stories rather than science and for being more sensationalist, as exemplified by programmes such as 'How to Kill a Human Being' presented by Michael Portillo, an ex-politician, minor celebrity and non-scientist, which investigates the death penalty and 'Chimps are Humans Too' presented by non-scientist Danny Wallace promoting his personal thesis that, as chimpanzees are genetically very close to human beings, they deserve similar rights and protection. Both programmes included considerable science but also were designed to cater for an audience familiar with a more sensationalist, celebrity-driven approach.

There is little doubt that *Horizon* has changed. And it is easy to see current editions as very different to the more Reithian approach taken by the programme in the 1970s and 80s. The debate over these changes is for another forum but an important point emerges from it. *Horizon* is particularly respected by many scientists who watched it when young. These individuals are, at the time of writing, often in senior positions within science. I have personal experience of some very senior scientists telling me that Horizon has 'gone off the boil,' is 'sensationalist' and 'not what it used to be'. That may be the case but many other aspects of society have also changed, and, to some extent, this criticism misses the point of modern broadcasting. It is not to educate or inform, but to attract an audience and as such must evolve with that audience. Even within a public service broadcaster like the BBC with a remit for education, every programme lives or dies by the number of viewers or listeners it gets.

Telling a story

All broadcasts from 45-second news items to hour-long documentaries tell a story. The item has to flow smoothly from start to finish. Any unexpected jumps can break the flow and lose the viewer or listener. That's not to say twists and turns cannot be used, they should be where appropriate, but care has to be taken to make sure that the audience is still gripped.

The simplest narrative style is the news story. Short and to the point, it follows a straightforward, linear structure of who did what, when, where, why and how, though not necessarily in that order. A longer item, perhaps a 4-minute report in a magazine programme, allows for a little more suspense and playing with the format. The story may start with outlining a problem and then take the audience through the process of working it out with the main findings at the end of the item, rather than at the beginning in a news story. A feature or documentary allows the programme maker to take the audience along a much longer, and more convoluted, journey. They can explore twists and turns and blind alleys but always need to return to the main thread running through the programme. A common device is to re-iterate the basic theme at regular intervals; this is particularly noticeable in programmes interrupted with advertising, the narrator inevitably gives a rehash of the story immediately after the commercial break.

One of the challenges and excitements of programme production is to take this very simple basic storytelling idea and re-work it. It may not appear as if there is much scope for originality given the need to tell a linear story, but there is always room for innovation. For example, who is telling the story? Is it a first person account told by the protagonist or a third person narrative told by an anonymous voice-over? Is it a montage with no linking narration, or largely narration over illustrative pictures? Is it a purely objective report, or is it an authored piece with the reporter adding his/her own views and ideas into the mix? Is it sympathetic to the plotline, or is it a confrontational piece designed to probe a misdemeanour or fraud?

Types of broadcaster

Broadly speaking there are two types of broadcaster, public sector and commercial. Commercial broadcasters have a relatively simple funding model. They put on programmes that draw an audience, and sell air-time within those programmes to companies wishing to advertise their products. The amount of money they can demand depends mainly on the size of the audience, and to a lesser extent the perceived buying power of that audience. Advertising is a constant struggle between the broadcaster attempting to get the biggest income and the advertiser trying to maximize their sales for the minimum outlay on adverts. Nevertheless, anyone who wants to put science on a commercial station needs to tackle this relationship.

Public sector broadcasting is funded by a number of different routes. In the United Kingdom, everyone who owns a television is required to buy a TV licence, the income from which goes to the BBC. The BBC World Service on the other hand is funded by a direct government grant. National Public Radio and Public TV channels in the United States are funded by donations from the public and run regular fund-raising events. Most countries have some state-run channels.

It is crucial, too, to remember that broadcasters live or die by the audience they attract. The reasons for wanting listeners may vary from the straightforward commercial need to sell advertising, to the more subtle requirements of ensuring that funders feel they are getting value for money. Whatever the reason, if you do not get an audience you are doomed.

Science, like every other topic, is used to draw and attract an audience. Some broadcasters will make it a strong element, others see it as a source of trivia, others still might ignore it all together. There are no hard and fast rules, and even if there were they would be revised constantly. The best way of discovering a broadcaster's attitude to science is to watch or listen. In fact, anyone who has any serious interest in broadcasting science has to watch and listen to a lot of programmes. Virtually all science broadcasters listen or watch almost obsessively, if you want to join them you will need to do the same.

Programme genres

Broadcasters are constantly working to come up with new programme formats in the hope of winning a bigger audience. In fact formats can be copyrighted and finding a winning format is a way to make big money by franchising it internationally. Look at *Big Brother* or *Who Wants to be a Millionaire?* for example. Nevertheless, even with all the ingenuity and effort applied there is only a small number of genre which features any significant science.

News
Fast moving with a very rapid turn around, news programming is the home of the adrenalin junky. Most broadcasters have regular bulletins at fixed times. However, the advent of rolling 24-hour news means that stories can be put on air at any time.

News tends to have a relatively large audience and one important point to remember is that news journalists listen to the stories broadcast by other news journalists. A small item on a local radio station may well be picked up by national TV and radio quite quickly, resulting in a deluge of requests. This can be a little overwhelming, so be prepared for your story to snowball.

Deadlines in news can be very short; it's not uncommon for a journalist to be on air half an hour or even less after encountering a story for the first time. However, much of the time, at least in science broadcasting, there is a little more time available. The main reason is that most of the big science stories come from embargoed press releases. For details of press releases and embargoes see Chapter 4.

Broadcast news journalism can be seen by others as rather shallow. There is little scope for depth and background in a 60-second news item and the medium is ephemeral. Crudely put, today's news is tomorrow's fish and chips wrapper – or whatever the broadcast version of a chip wrapper might be.

News has to be new and there is a detailed discussion of it in the Chapter 4. However, it is worth noting that TV needs pictures and the chances of something getting to air are greatly enhanced if there are dramatic pictures to back it up.

Magazine

Magazine programmes tend to be current, but are not driven solely by the news agenda. They are made up of a mix of different items. Science items may appear in dedicated science programmes or in more general offerings such as early evening news magazines. The pace is slightly less rushed than a news item and will typically explore a little more background and implications of the science under discussion. An item may last anywhere between 2 and 10 minutes, though 3–6 is more usual.

It is rare for the producers of a magazine programme to be content with a quick phone call to a contributor. Most of the time a producer, presenter or reporter will visit the interviewee or will ask them to come in to a studio. It might be the main studio from where the programme is broadcast or it might be a remote studio connected by a high quality audio or video feed.

Story selection is hugely variable depending on the type of programme but it's likely that at least one, often most, will be based on a current item such as the publication of a research paper. Other stories will be sourced by the producer, researcher or reporter perhaps by running through their contacts or just cold calling. However, the majority will be the result of a press release or an organization directly contacting the programme makers.

There are a number of different possible structures for a magazine item: a straight one to one interview, a discussion with more than one contributor, a package of pre-recorded segments linked together by script. They may employ sound or visual effects and often include music. One of the challenges of producing such a programme is to stretch the magazine format and develop novel production ideas. These can include regular slots of a similar sort, short news type bulletins or whatever else the creative juices come up with. Magazine programmes allow you to try out ideas without committing an entire programme's resources to an untested approach.

Documentary/features

The lengths and formats vary but this style of programme explores one subject in depth. They are always pre-recorded and in the case of TV, contributors may spend days or even weeks being filmed. For example, a crew may follow researchers on a long field trip or the researchers themselves may be asked to record a video or audio diary over a period of many months.

There are number of different approaches to making a long documentary, some of which are touched up on in the section Telling a Story above.

It is crucial that the producer decide on the approach before starting to film or record. Will it have a narrator? Will the story be told in the first or third person?

The classic style is to record events and interviews with the contributors, determine a story line, edit the material into that story and link it all together with a narrated script. This is a highly flexible format which allows the producer scope to tell the story in the way most suited to their audience. It allows for last-minute changes and updates as these can be incorporated into the script at the final stages of production. A good example of this is the Horizon's 'Fermat's Last Theorem'.

A variation on this theme is the authored film, whereby a presenter tells a personal story and injects his/her own views and ideas into the narration. The challenge here is to find a presenter with a good story to tell and the ability to tell it. While many scientists have great stories to tell, they may not always be great storytellers.

A more challenging approach is the montage. No narration is used and the story is told by intercutting interviews with the contributors, and perhaps a presenter recorded on location. It can be very effective but requires considerable thought and planning. It has to be possible to edit the story from the recorded interviews and so every angle needs to be covered when recording or filming.

Making such a programme is invariably a complex and difficult business. To make it work it needs to have a coherent story line running through it, albeit one that inevitably changes as recording and editing progresses. Documentaries and features are seen as the pinnacle of factual broadcasting.

Fiction

While the vast majority of science broadcasting is necessarily factual, there are times when fiction is used to great effect. One example of this is the dramatic reconstruction. The cameras and microphones were not there at the initial event so the production crew re-create them. One of the best examples of this was the BBC *Horizon* special Life Story that dramatized the discovery of the structure of DNA by Crick, Watson, Wilkins and Franklin. It was, effectively, a feature film and required a large budget and considerable production effort – and is a relatively rare occurrence as a result.

Science also appears to greater or lesser extent in purely fictional programmes. For example, *The Simpsons* have included accurate descriptions of some scientific principles and even an appearance by the physicist Steven Hawking. Science consultants are sometimes involved in these productions, as they are on some Hollywood films. The scientist will not appear on camera and may not even get a credit but it is a way that science can make it into broadcasting. Particularly with fictional programmes there can be a tension between the accuracy of the science and the dramatic requirements of the programme. Drama deliberately takes current knowledge and expands it, or distorts it, depending on your perspective.

Getting a story to air

This section turns to practical guidance on getting to air from the first identi-fication of a story through to the broadcast itself.

What makes a good story?
This is one of the hardest questions to answer. A good story will be engaging, perhaps informative, often entertaining and may well be amusing, horrifying or enthralling. Some stories, such as the cloning of Dolly the Sheep, leap out from the page and are obvious. Others, such as the discovery of a new type of plastic, may need teasing out and exploring before its story value becomes apparent. The new type of plastic could well be the basis of cheap, water resistant, electronics making a whole new industry possible, for example.

A very crude, three word, maxim explains the nature of at least one type of story: sex, death and bodily functions. That is, if the research illuminates any facet of reproduction, disease and suffering, then it is likely to add up to a story. Relating the research to human experience is a classic way of put-ting a story across and the sex, death and bodily functions test is a quick way of determining whether it will work. All health and medicine stories fit. So do stories about early human ancestors – where did we come from is a sex-related question albeit not to the act but to the principle of procreation. Environmental stories, particularly doom-laden ones, clearly fall into the death category. But what about, say astronomy? The search for a start and end to the Universe fits very neatly into sex and death. Life on other planets – the 'are we alone' question – always gets extensive coverage. And astronauts are constantly asked how they go to the toilet in space.

Another broad category of story that often makes it into the media is just the curious or the interesting – the sort of titbit that is swapped in bars and cafes around the world. The discovery of a new type of dinosaur is always grist for the media mill as is the discovery of a new species of mammal, an interesting fact in its own right.

The solution to Fermat's last theorem was well reported. It's an interesting piece of maths but not directly relevant to everyday life and only really com-prehensible to a very small number of mathematicians. Yet it was extensively covered largely because of the good personal story of the mathematician who had dedicated his life to its solution. This last leads on to another important element of storytelling in the popular media, the human angle.

One year, at the annual festival of the British Association for the Advancement of Science there was a lecture given by a researcher on sea-horses. Seahorses are not necessarily particularly noteworthy, though it was an interesting piece of research, yet the research made it into every broadsheet and also onto TV. Why? Because the researcher just happened to be a highly attractive, blond woman who was happy to do photoshoots. While there is no firm evidence that this is the sole reason – the newspapers could all have decided that seahorses were 'in' – an informal and off the record canvass of other journalists suggested they believed her looks played a part.

This does make the media appear a little shallow, suggesting that a pretty face is a substitute for a good story. Well, in part, it is. And whether you like it or not it does pay to be aware of this. But look a little deeper and the situation is more complex. Research by itself is fascinating to the researcher but the way it is presented to the outside world is via dry, third person accounts in peer reviewed journals (see Chapter 4). Both radio and TV are intimate media, personal stories work very well whereas regurgitation of facts is a turn-off for all but the very few. One of the most important tools in the producer's repertoire is finding an angle on the scientist behind the story. What are their ups and downs? Are they embroiled in a particularly bitter academic tussle? Are they mavericks challenging the established consensus? Any of these elements can be used to increase the appeal of a particular story.

Charities are very good at this. Whenever they launch a new fund-raising appeal they always make sure that someone who has benefited from their work is available to give interviews. Likewise when a group of researchers makes a breakthrough to help cure a particular disease, the press release is often accompanied by details of patients available for interview.

Sources

Crudely speaking there are two ways a story idea reaches a producer. They receive some sort of notification, usually a press release, or they find it themselves. With the large, and increasing, pressures on producers, there is normally very little time to source all stories from their own contacts. Most come from some form of press release. For ideas on writing and using press releases, see Pitching a story in Chapter 4.

How you pitch a story idea to the broadcast media depends largely on the type of programme. A news or magazine programme producer will received hundreds of press releases a day and will sift through them for story ideas. They will probably make the choice as to which stories to broadcast and just run them past the programme or news editor to confirm. It can be a very quick process and with news in particular things can happen very fast.

Pitching a story into this environment can be tricky. Good advice is to phone first and have an email ready written to send off to the producer or journalist as soon as you put the phone down. Think the story through carefully beforehand, for you will have probably less than thirty seconds to grab the broadcaster's attention. Think about what time of day you make the contact. If you want to talk with a news desk find out what time the regular bulletins go out and get in touch a long time before or just after they have finished. Calling five minutes before a bulletin is due on air will get you short shrift.

Think about the points you wish to make, two or three at most, and how they relate to the audience's experience, if they do. If you have a good environment to film or record in, something interesting to hear or see, say so. If it is relevant, give an idea of the potential impact of the research. For example, the identification of a gene for a crippling disease is interesting from the research point of view but it may be relevant to people with the disease as it could point towards a potential treatment. Similarly, a new way of removing carbon dioxide from power station flue gasses could lead to a cheap way of burning coal without releasing climate change-inducing carbon dioxide into the atmosphere. However, be careful not to over exaggerate the potential benefits. If you say you have a cure for the common cold then its best to really have one rather than just the potential.

Be friendly and be prepared to be flexible. If the producer wants you to travel to a studio then do so. Clear some time so that if they want to visit you to film that afternoon they can do so. Be prepared for the arrangements to chop and change and only think it is over when the programme has been broadcast.

At the other end of the spectrum are major features and documentaries. It can take weeks, if not months, of research to settle on a story for one of these. The process involves hours and hours of research and phone conversations. Many people will be involved in the final choice of story: researchers, producers, series producers, series editors and very possibly the commissioning editors and network controllers. Pitching a story into this environment involves, in part, finding and developing a relationship with a working producer or researcher. It may be that you talk with them occasionally over months or years before anything comes to fruition.

BOX 5.2   CASE STUDY: PITCHING IDEAS

The fictional stories below illustrate two different pitches, one for news and one for a documentary. This story would be pitched in autumn 2008 when MRSA infections in hospitals around the world are of great concern.

News pitch

Super antibiotic discovered – the end for MRSA
A new type of antibiotic that turns bacteria against themselves could mean the end to lethal MRSA infections. After 20 years of research, scientists at the University of Bacton have found a chemical that makes the bacteria self-destruct. It can kill MRSA while leaving human cells intact in the test tube. Professor Dilys Cottells, who discovered the chemical called Bacterial Suicide Inducing Factor or BSIF, said 'MRSA kills thousands of people each year, mainly children and elderly. We hope to be able to use BSIF to tackle infections and save many lives.' Professor Cottells is available for interview.

Feature pitch

The woman who will save thousands
This is the story of a dogged scientist who refused to give up in the face of disbelief and professional scepticism. And now that tenacious researcher could lift one of the biggest threats to hospital patients, the spectre of dying of MRSA.

Thirty years ago a young graduate student called Dilys Cottells spotted something odd in one of her test tubes. The bacteria she was growing seemed to commit mass suicide. This was not part of her PhD work on the genetics of Staphylococcus and her supervisor discouraged her from pursuing it. Reluctantly she did, but it never left her thoughts. For ten years she worked hard at her genetics and became one of the rising stars of the field. Eventually she was able to persuade the University of Bacton to give her a small grant to pursue her suicidal bacteria. It was slow work, she could only spend one day a week on it at best, and everyone around her thought she was chasing ghosts.

Those ghosts came to life nearly 10 years later. By this time hospitals were becoming very concerned about a new antibiotic resistant bacterium that was killing vulnerable patients. Called MRSA, it could only be killed by a single antibiotic, and if it became resistant to that then there was nothing that could stop it. In the mean time Cottell's work had taken her away from Staphylococcus into the genetics of methane-producing bacteria. But a chance meeting with a hospital doctor on a train convinced her to return to her suicidal bacteria. Working alone and at night, she took just five years to isolate the chemical that induced the bacteria to kill themselves, and today she is being hailed as the saviour of hospitals around the world.

Working in the broadcast media

Roles in broadcasting

Broadcasting is a team effort. At times the team is very small – such as a radio programme produced and presented by one individual. In this case, the teamwork relies on working with the contributors and the engineers, executives and administrators who put the programme on air. At the other end of the spectrum a major TV series can have fifty or so individuals all working towards the same goal, a seamless, fluent broadcast. There are similar roles in both radio and TV but they often have different names and different responsibilities. While many people have careers that span both media, it's important to recognize the differences between the two. And as is always the case when talking about something as complex as broadcasting, the outlines below are guidelines and not hard-and-fast rules.

Controller or channel editor
This person has overall responsibility for deciding what programmes run on their channel, and it is *their* channel. Controllers succeed or fail on their ability to provide a mix of programmes that draw in and keep an audience. The controller, or editor, is crucially important in the work of a producer. Put bluntly, if a producer does not please a controller then he does not get to make many programmes. The relationship is of course much more subtle than that but it's crucial to remember the power that controllers and editors have.

Presenter

As the voice or face of the programme the presenter is the link between listener or viewer and the content and as a result a programme normally has only one or at most a small pool of presenters. While a programme may have many producers in its lifetime, the turnover of presenters is likely to be much lower. Presenter's involvement with the programme varies dramatically. Sometimes they are deeply involved from start to finish, other times they may only appear right at the end to read the script.

Script reading is the most basic job of the presenter, linking the individual elements of the programme, knitting it into a coherent whole. This is quite a skill. It is not easy to read from a text and make it sound conversational and spontaneous. They will need to sound comfortable doing so for radio and appear relaxed in front of a camera for TV. Unsurprisingly, good presenters are in demand.

In radio, presenters normally have a significant input into the script, often writing it in its entirety. This is less common in TV but in all cases the presenter needs to be well briefed by the producer. That may be easy if the presenter was involved from the beginning, but that is rarely the case, so good communication between presenter and producer is essential. Another key role of the presenter is to interview the contributors, either live on air or pre-recorded. As with reading a script, this is deceptively tricky. A skilled interviewer needs to listen, think on their feet, be well briefed on the topic and able, during the interview, to take directions from a producer through their headphones or earpiece.

In both TV and radio, presenters can be either freelance or members of staff. They will often have a high profile, working across many formats and doing other jobs such as chairing public meetings or appearing as guests on other programmes. This can make working with high-profile presenters a challenge; they may have very little time to offer a broadcaster so the producer has to be skilled in working around them.

Reporter

This role is most common in news and current affairs, though many magazine programmes also have reporters. Their job is to report on events on location (i.e., outside the studio). Radio reporters often record and edit their own interviews, giving the producer a nearly complete package ready for final polishing before being inserted into the programme. This is rarer in TV but with the advent of small, cheap digital cameras increasing numbers of reporters do just that. Like the presenter, reporters help to form the sound, appearance and character of the programme and good ones are in demand. Many reporters go on to be producers or presenters.

Producer

The producer has the most wide ranging role, the hardest to define and the most important. The exact nature of the job varies depending on the programme but, put simply, the producer brings all the elements together to make the programme happen. In radio this can be virtually everything, recording, editing, directing, script writing, but the complexity of TV requires more people to be involved.

Producers may be responsible for an individual programme or for coordinating an entire series of programmes. There are also the executive producers who oversee programmes but are not normally involved in the day to day production tasks. You may also encounter variants such as development producer, responsible for developing new programme ideas.

A producer will choose the stories to cover, line up the interviewees, supervise the interviews and often conduct them, determine the running order, produce the script outline or write the entire script, write the trails, produce publicity material, direct the studio, ensure the final programme is the correct length and fulfils the programme brief. On top of that they will respond to listeners and viewers queries; deal with any complaints and be held responsible for any and everything to do with the programme.

A producer needs a good understanding of recording techniques and radio producers must be able to use a basic recording studio and portable recording equipment in the field. They will also need to be able to edit their recordings, normally on a computer. A good producer will also have a clear idea of how the programme will be put together and how it will sound overall. Essentially they need to be a good story-teller. A crucial element of production is working with different people. Contributors need to be persuaded to take part, presenters need to be briefed and there needs to be a significant amount of liaison with the rest of the broadcasting organization in order to ensure that the programme gets to air.

Researcher

Their job, as the description suggests, is to find content for the programme under the direction of the producer. This will range from trawling literature and websites for ideas or contributors and long conversations with potential contributors, to fact checking and talking with phone-in guests just before they go on air. Many researchers will also be asked to record interviews from time to time as well as help out with most of the other production tasks and roles. A researcher may also work across a number of different programmes simultaneously. A science radio unit may, for example, have one researcher responsible for keeping all producers fed with the latest information. As much of their job requires persuading people to give up their time, researchers need good people skills.

TV researchers may also find locations and track down props. There are also specific jobs for film and picture researchers who will wade through mountains of tapes and pictures to find the right one to illustrate a particular idea for the programme.

Broadcast assistant/production assistant

There are many different names for this role but typically the job is to provide administrative support for the programme. There is always some paperwork required, lists of programme content and contributors need to be filed and so on. A broadcast assistant may also do some elements of research and production. They could, for example, be asked to line up a contributor on a particular topic or record an interview if the producer was tied up elsewhere. Typically, a broadcast assistant would work across a number of programmes simultaneously.

Director

TV programmes, particularly documentaries, often have a director as well as a producer. Responsible for the look of the programme, directors will choose the shots, the camera angles and any special effects that are required in the filming. A good director will always work closely with the camera operator, whose skill and experience they will use to complement their own.

Programme making skills

Interviewing

A good description of an interview is that it is a guided conversation. The interviewer knows the basic direction of the discussion and also some specific points that they want to draw out but is open enough to explore other interesting areas as they arise. Good interviewers can make the whole process sound deceptively simple, just chatting. To get to that point takes practice and then more practice.

Both TV and Radio use two types of interviews: live and pre-recorded. Live recordings are made while the programme is on air, whereas a pre-recorded interview is recorded in advance and edited in the studio. Some programmes use a mix of live and pre-recorded interviews, while others will be recorded live in their entirety or completely pre-recorded.

Live programmes

Live interviews might seem more challenging than pre-recorded interviews but with proper preparation, they are no harder and can actually draw a better performance from both presenter and contributors. From a broadcaster's point of view, live interviews add an element of unpredictability to the programme which is exciting for both the production team and the viewers or listeners. From the contributor's point of view, it affords them total control over what they say and the knowledge that their words will not be edited or taken out of context.

For live programming, preparation is all – by everyone concerned. If it is to be a short news interview then the presenter will need a thorough brief from the producer. The contributor will need to establish two or three points that they wish to make and have any analogies or explanations prepared and rehearsed. For longer discussion programmes the presenter will have prepared a script – or at the very least, comprehensive notes – that provide an overall structure. Everyone involved should have a copy of this structure so there are not too many surprises. Live programming benefits from a little uncertainty, but will fall apart if no-one is there to keep the conversation going in the right direction.

Pre-recorded programmes

There are numerous different ways to pre-record an interview for use in a programme. The contributors may be in a studio alongside the interviewer or they could be in a remote studio – sitting in a small box in front of a camera or microphone. Alternatively the interview could take place on location, either at the contributor's workplace or in another location relevant to the topic under discussion.

If the recording is made on location then the producer will want to hear or see something interesting, either as a demonstration or in the background. There is no point leaving the controlled situation of a studio to go to another neutral, clean sounding room. Background activity sets a scene and adds a context to the programme. It's far more interesting to see a metallurgist talking about his/her work surrounded by furnaces and microscopes than sitting in a studio.

Pre-recorded interviews are always edited. This allows a considerable degree of freedom to record different versions, to repeat the sequence until it is correct and to edit the programme together in the most effective way.

One of the main considerations when out recording or filming on location is to make sure that you have all the material you need. The time taken and cost involved in getting everyone together with all the right equipment means that going back again is almost always impossible. Much of the interview may be background that could be used in structuring the programme and writing the script. A producer may have an idea that is discarded in the editing suite. Whatever the reason, it is always better to have too much than too little, though far too much does make the editing process a lot harder.

Radio location recording can be relatively straightforward. Interviews are recorded onto compact portable equipment. Walking and talking is possible, as is moving from room to room or showing the interviewer an example of what the contributor is talking about. There will be a little disruption to the local environment, such as turning off radios and asking people not to talk too loudly in the background, but overall it is a minimally invasive process.

Location filming can be relatively straightforward but more often than not it does require a reasonable amount of setting up. Lighting is crucial, and rigging even a simple two light set up may easily take half an hour or more. Then there is the exact camera angle and effect the director requires. Any props need to be to hand and the interviewee will need to have a microphone clipped on and checked. The cameras themselves can be bulky and every new shot requires them to be moved. The effort needed to produce a short segment of TV often seems disproportional. But it needs to be, cameras can only record what is placed in front of them and even the slightest change requires a new setup.

Editing

Editing is a time consuming and difficult skill to acquire, but developing it is essential for any programme maker. There are no hard and fast rules to editing, just use the material you have available to tell the best story you are able.

The editing process is designed to extract a key story from a longer conversation and do so in a way that appears natural and seamless. From a practical point of view there are a number of things to consider including the intonation of a person's voice, the background noise, the quality of the recording.

The bigger intangible with editing is deciding what to keep in and what to leave out. You will have an idea of what story you want to tell, so it will be relatively easy to discard some of the preamble and irrelevant stuff. The chances are, though, that you will still be left with far more than you have space to include. So here are a couple of tips.

Descriptions in interviews are often long and rambling; it is almost always possible to write a shorter description in the script. By combining careful scripting with a small amount of the interview it is possible to give the emphasis to the interviewee but write a clear explanation in the script.

No-one but you knows what you leave on the cutting room floor. There may be reams of excellent, fascinating material but if it does not serve your purpose cut it out. In some circumstances, particularly if you are under pressure of time, then simply stop when you have enough! It may seem like sacrilege to deliberately ignore a chunk of interview, but if you are on air in fifteen minutes, that's what you've got to do.

Overall, editing requires practice. It can seem daunting to try and turn fifteen hours of recording into a half hour programme, but think of the story. Always think of the story you are telling and in time it will get easier.

Scripting

Even though it may not sound like it, all TV and radio programmes are scripted to a lesser or greater extent. Script writing is an art and very different from either formal academic writing or writing in the popular media. A script is meant to be read aloud and sound like natural speech.

A good script will guide the viewer or listener through the programme, giving them enough information to prepare for what the interviewees will say but not give the game away. The classic way of doing this is to find a subject that is either topical or relevant to which many of the audience can relate. For example, if you are introducing a piece on the discovery of a new galaxy you may start by saying, 'If you stare into the sky on a dark, clear night you may see many thousands of stars.' Then take the audience through the idea that they are just seeing stars from our own galaxy, the Milky Way then finally introduce the idea that there are many millions of galaxies. It is all about making sure the audience is prepared for what is coming next.

A script may well repeat or paraphrase an important point and will, of course, make sure the contributors are introduced with the proper name and title. The script will be the last thing prepared before going into the studio as it has to fit with the finished audio. And in a live programme, particularly news programmes, the presenter will need to be adept at last-minute changes, often given seconds before over their headphones by a busy producer. When writing for radio it's worth noting that normal speech is about 150 to 180 words per minute for English, which is not very much at all.

When writing a TV script there is the additional challenge of complementing the pictures. It is no good just describing what is on screen, a common trap for beginners. The voice-over needs, like radio, to make sure the audience is prepared for what is coming next and to reinforce any key points. A past master at this is David Attenborough. His scripts and delivery are deceptively simple, adding to what is playing out on screen without ever taking over.

Editorial control

Perhaps one of the most common questions asked of producers by contributors is 'can I see it before it goes out?' The usual answer is, and should be, no. This is often greeted with some bafflement, the contributor gave the interview willingly so why can they not have a say in how it is edited? The answer is twofold.

First the production crew are the experts in making programmes. By taking part you are allowing them to make the final decisions about how your contribution will be used. They have a good understanding of the audience and all the other factors such as the time of broadcast and what other programmes on similar subjects might also be going out. They also have the ultimate responsibility for the content of the programme and cannot hand that over to anyone else.

Second, it is a matter of the freedom of the press, broadcast or other media, that is, a matter of principle. Ceding control to a contributor risks compromising journalistic independence or risks allowing a programme to be biased in some specific direction.[1]

There are times when the programme maker may want to check facts or if it is a particularly sensitive topic then they may agree to preview it with the interviewees. This, though, is purely fact checking and not an opportunity for the interviewee to comment on the style or content of the programme.

New technologies

Ever since the advent of broadcasting, the challenge for anyone wanting to make radio or TV programmes has been getting access to the airwaves. Licensing was introduced in the earliest days of radio, and most countries continue to have some sort of licensing system for broadcasters. To go on air without a licence is normally illegal. Today, though, a new type of broadcasting is available without a need for a licence, just a computer and Internet access.

Combine this with the development of cheap, good quality cameras, recorders and computer based editing and what was once the preserve of privileged broadcasters is becoming available to keen amateurs. There is the challenge of getting and audience for your work, simply placing a small film on a website does not mean people will find it and watch it. But there are ways and means of doing so.

Downloading and streaming

TV and audio can be gathered from a website in two basic ways. The simplest is a file that is offered for download. A surfer simply clicks on the file, it is downloaded to their computer and they can play it at their leisure. The disadvantage of this is that the files can be very large and take a long time to download and can only be watched after the transfer is complete.

The alternative to downloading is streaming. Here an audio or video file is sent in a continuous stream to an individual's computer and played as it arrives much like a conventional broadcast. The disadvantage of this is that it is not as easy to listen to or watch the programmes away from an Internet connection. It is possible to download and save streamed programmes but it is not always easy and normally requires third party programmes and reasonable computing skills.

Digital rights management (DRM)

Broadcasters, film makers, writers and producers make their income from selling the programmes they make. There is a great deal of concern about the theft of copyrighted material on the Internet and Digital Rights Management (DRM) is a technology, or rather a number of technologies, that have been developed to prevent this. The principle is that embedded within the audio or video is a code that prevents unauthorized playing of the material. So, for example, a person may pay for and download a piece of music to their computer but it might not be possible to play it on any other computer, preventing them from passing it on to their friends.

This is a complex subject, and a controversial one. The demise of DRM has been predicted on a number of occasions but at the moment it seems likely that anyone dealing with Internet broadcasting will need to have at least a passing knowledge of this area. It is unlikely to disappear completely in the near future.

Podcasting and vodcasting

Podcasts and vodcasts are, respectively, audio and video files that you can download from the Internet. They are specifically designed to be downloaded to a computer and then transferred to a portable audio or video device such as a Zen MP3 player or an Apple iPod. You can subscribe to a podcast or vodcast and every time a new one is available it will automatically be downloaded to your computer and then added to your portable device when you next connect it.

Invariably budding Internet broadcasters need to piggyback on an established website with a developed audience. For videos the most popular at present is *YouTube, http://www.youtube.com*. This is a commercial site that makes its money from advertising and provides a simple way of uploading your videos to the Internet. Once uploaded, the clips will be available to the millions of people who visit the site, and there is a record of how many times each clip is viewed. The real power of *YouTube* is the fact that you can include your video alongside other similar ones and the fact that users can search for clips with a specific content.

BOX 5.3   CASE STUDY: YOUTUBE

Take a look at the large number of science-related *YouTube* clips. There are videos of experiments that teachers can use in the classroom, university level descriptions of the double slit experiment demonstrating the unintuitive nature of quantum mechanics and wacky science related demonstrations such as the extraordinary reaction you get when the sweets Mentos are mixed with Diet Coke – explosive, informative and very entertaining.

A very different example comes from the 'Astrobiology Rap' composed and performed by Jonathan Chase, one of my ex-students. He was asked to write an astrobiology rap for NASA *Astrobiology* magazine. He did and put the video up on YouTube where it slowly gained a cult following. It was picked up by the BBC and Chase featured on a BBC morning magazine programme. He has performed it at the Science Museum in London and it's a pretty good start to a career in Science Communication; one that would have been impossible without the ability of the Internet to make and broadcast TV easily and cheaply.

Pod- and vod-casters can also register their programme with a larger organization and so increase the number of potential viewers and listeners. The leader at present is Apple iTunes. Anyone can register their podcast with iTunes, as long as it meets certain criteria, and anyone who subscribes to the iTunes store can access your podcast. Once again the podcast can be included alongside others of a similar nature, increasing their chances of being downloaded, and users can search using specific key words.

One of the major growth areas in Internet broadcasting is the number of traditionally print media who are producing podcasts and vodcasts. Most of the UK broadsheets offer podcasts of various types, including science. For example, *The Guardian* produces a weekly science podcast (http://www. blogs.guardian.co.uk/science/category/podcast_1/). *Nature*, the peer reviewed science journal, produces increasing numbers of podcasts and vodcasts (see http://www.nature.com/nature/podcast/) as does *New Scientist* (http://www. newscientist.com/podcast.ns).

Perhaps the most significant, and growing, area for science Internet broadcasting are the podcasts and vodcasts appearing on institutional websites. Many universities are producing podcasts as are organizations such as the Institute of Physics (http://podcasts.iop.org/) and the Royal Society (http://royalsociety.org/page.asp?id=3966). From a broadcasting point of view these tend to be rather crude. They are normally straight interviews or recordings of lectures with little editing or production. While interesting and informative, they are unlikely to garner a significant audience in this form. However, there is a huge potential to use the techniques of broadcast production to improve their quality and broaden their appeal.

Multimedia

This is a term frequently heard alongside any mention of Internet broadcasting. It's often used loosely and I have not found a satisfactory, consistent definition. It is normally used to mean that the Internet and other digital forms of publishing and broadcasting are able to deliver a variety of different media forms simultaneously. For example it is possible to run a slide show with an audio commentary, or a video alongside a more detailed text based description of the video content. This is powerful and in particular it allows a digital broadcaster to appeal to different audiences simultaneously. A younger, casual audience may want short, exciting video clips whereas an audience of students may want more in-depth information. Yet another audience may want a podcast to download and listen to on the move.

It is clear that this approach has a great deal of potential, but also a considerable number of pitfalls. Part of the reason for the lack of a good definition of multimedia is that to date multimedia is not a distinct media form. Nothing has yet emerged that is not a combination of text; audio; video and pictures. There are certainly examples of their innovative use but they are, still, just combinations of pre-digital media forms.

There are, though, some areas where you can start to see glimmers of new media forms, media that are only possible with digital delivery. Blogs and message boards provide for rapid conversations and sharing of ideas. Instant messaging allows not only the transfer of instant messages but also pictures, videos and audio, both live and pre-recorded. Webcasts are used for a huge variety of different purposes from press conferences to university lectures. It's possible to see how a combination of these different means of delivery will result in genuinely new forms of broadcasting. For example, a live webcast could be viewed and supplemental material in the form of text, videos or audio clips sent at the same time for later reference, or perhaps a system of discussing and sharing ideas with a common area of the screen set out for people to present data in whatever form for discussion.

The pace of innovation is startling and new ideas are emerging all the time. However, at the moment they all require some elements of the more traditional communication skills. Video and audio production; script writing;

storytelling and straight old-fashioned journalism. I am certain that the science broadcaster of the future will use a very different set of tools, and have different ways to connecting to their audience. It is unlikely that they will be able to abandon the principles of science broadcasting entirely. The world will always need storytellers.

Conclusion

Science broadcasting is an important, exciting and rapidly developing area of science communication. In essence it is storytelling. A good story well told makes for a compelling programme and most people have their favourites. It's hard to say what is a good programme or what is a poor one as so much of the definition of good and bad is subjective. And trying to give examples of such programmes in a book is virtually impossible; a programme derives much of its impact from the fact that it is listened to and watched rather than read.

There is always scope for more and better science programming. I believe that the Internet will allow talented novices to show their wares whereas traditionally it has been difficult to break into broadcasting. Not everyone can make programmes, it is difficult. Not everyone is a good interviewer; that takes confidence and practice. However, there is no way of finding out unless you try. So if you are a scientist or science communicator, get yourself on air, you may find you have an ability to open your field of science to a much larger audience. And if you feel like making a programme, borrow a portable MP3 recorder and have a go. It is fun and you could be embarking on a whole new career.

Note

1. That there are other threats to journalistic independence is a discussion beyond the scope of this chapter.

ACTIVITIES

■ As an exercise try fitting any science stories you see or hear on TV or radio into one of these categories: sex, death or bodily functions. Don't take it too literally; this is designed to get you thinking about story angles.

■ Find a science story in a magazine or newspaper. Write a brief script for an imaginary 15-minute feature on the topic. Now boil it down to a 45-second news item.

■ Imagine you are the producer of a magazine programme. You have 4 items and need one more. The current stories concern a new gene for cancer; a new estimate of the numbers of species living in the rainforest; the latest results from the Large Hadron Collider at CERN announced just this week and an update on the development of a new drug. Put these stories in the best order for the programme and find a fifth story to go with them.

References and further reading

Barnouw, E. (1966), *A History of Broadcasting in the United States: a tower in Babel Vol 1. To 1933*. Oxford University Press (New York).

Briggs, A. (1985), *The BBC: The First Fifty Years*. Oxford University Press (Oxford).

Day, P. (1994), *The Radio Years: A History of Broadcasting in New Zealand Vol 1*. Auckland University Press (Auckland).

Endén, R. (1996), *Yleisradio 1926–1996: A History of Broadcasting in Finland*, Finnish Historical Society (Helsinki).

Pegg, M. (1983), *Broadcasting and Society 1918–1939*. Croom Helm (London).

Priestman, C. (2001), Web Radio: Radio Production for Internet Streaming. Focal Press (St Louis, MO).

Presenting Science

Karen Bultitude

6

This chapter provides an overview of how to effectively present scientific concepts to a live audience. Whilst the presentation itself may take on a variety of different formats (e.g., a poster, lecture, demonstration or wider discussion), the crucial common element is that of recognizing and catering for different *audiences*. This chapter outlines how to both define and target audiences – ideas which will run as consistent themes throughout the rest of the book. Common motivations for both individuals and institutions involved in presenting science are outlined, as are different methods of communicating directly with a live audience.

LEARNING POINTS

Theoretical learning points

- Defining and catering for different audiences

Practical learning points

- Planning and preparation
- Presentation and facilitation skills
- Creating presentation slides and other resources
- Dos and Don'ts of live experiments and demonstrations
- Reflection and evaluation

Introduction

Methods of communicating *directly* with public audiences are considered within this chapter. This occurs most commonly via some form of interactive activity with a live audience. The comparative advantages and disadvantages

Table 6.1 Comparative advantages and disadvantages of presenting science either directly to an audience or via media channels

Direct (live) intervention		Media intervention	
Pros	Cons	Pros	Cons
Audience personally meet a scientist	Small audience size	Reach a large potential audience	Scientist no longer has control over what is delivered
Scientist has control of content	Resource (time, money) intensive; low sustainability	Opinion formers/ decision makers likely to be in the audience	Limited focus, both in time and subject matter
Two-way communication is possible	Often preaching to the converted	Different media have different audience profiles so targeting is possible	Generally one-way communication

of communicating science to a live public audience, rather than via various media channels, are outlined in Table 6.1.

When deciding how to communicate a scientific message to a public audience it is important to keep clearly in mind the aims and intentions of the communication; if a large potential audience is crucial then a media intervention may be the only suitable method. However if the initiative seeks to discern audience attitudes then a two-way communication method is preferable, thereby requiring some sort of personal contact with the audience. This chapter focuses specifically on the skills and resources appropriate to presenting science directly to a public audience.

Motivations for presenting science in public

Every science communication practitioner, whether they are professional or amateur, will have his/her own individual mix of personal and professional reasons for wanting to communicate science directly to public audiences. There is no doubt that most presenters find science communication rewarding and fulfilling, obtaining a great deal of enjoyment out of their experience. Others feel a strong passion for their chosen scientific discipline, and a need to share that passion with others. From a professional perspective the most commonly cited reasons are to:

- ensure that science and technology are an integral part of everyday experience;
- produce a science and technology literate workforce; and to
- enable citizens to play an informed role in their democracy

In the case of certain activities (such as the Royal Institution of Great Britain's annual Christmas Lectures) there is a great deal of prestige associated

with being chosen to present the activity. Many teachers and university lecturers see science communication as a natural extension of their normal jobs,
aiming to improve recruitment and interest in their subject. Increasingly, funding bodies and institutions are acknowledging a need to communicate about
their research as part of a recognition that the public have a right to know
about work that is publicly funded.

Catering for different audiences

Arguably, the most important principle in science communication is audience
targeting. At its most simplistic, the audience is the group of people to *whom*
the scientific message is being communicated. The audience is often closely
related to the location at which the event occurs; the people who are physically in the vicinity (e.g., the individuals located within a lecture theatre or the
people who shop at a particular shopping mall). By considering the audience
in terms of the event location it is possible to make some assumptions about
their background. For example, an event held in a lecture theatre is likely to
recruit people who are relatively educated (and therefore comfortable with
attending a lecture theatre) and will have actively chosen to attend (since it is
unlikely that people will be present at a lecture theatre by chance). Similarly,
key visitor demographics can often be obtained in advance from the management team at venues such as shopping centres. This information may provide
significant insights into the mindset of the intended audience.

Physical aspects of the venue will also influence interaction with the audience, affecting the format, duration, content and even level at which you
should pitch the event. Carefully considering these aspects together with
details of the likely audience will greatly increase the chances of producing a
successful event. In some cases you may wish to change the venue in order to
reach the audience you have in mind more effectively.

If the message (*what* is being communicated) and delivery medium (*how* it
is being communicated) are tailored so that they are of interest to the audience
and likely to capture their attention, the activity is more likely to be successful. However before adjusting the message or identifying the most appropriate
medium, you first need to understand exactly *who* the audience is. This section
outlines how audience characteristics may be identified, for example according
to demographics, attitudes or behaviours, and interests.

Why target the audience?

There is a wide variety of reasons to tailor the message to the audience. Some
of the most important are

- the message is more effective if linked to participant needs;
- participants have greater connection to the intervention/initiative since it is
  specifically designed to interest them; and

■ participants are more receptive since the content is at the appropriate level (e.g., doesn't patronize or insult, is not too difficult/easy etc.)

This is true not only for science communication, but also more widely, for example you would be unlikely to get the job if you sent the same CV and covering letter to different prospective employers. Each person involved wants to feel that you are interested in them as an individual (or in the case of the CV, in that specific job at that institution), and that you have made an effort to adapt your content in order to suit them best.

Defining the audience

There are a number of ways in which the collective features of an audience can be identified. In science communication the most commonly used characteristics are:

■ **Demographics:** e.g., by gender, race, age, income, education/ knowledge of a topic, or a combination of these. Breakdowns of this information for specific regions are often available from the office or bureau of national statistics within each country, for example http://www.abs.gov.au/ in Australia, http://www.statistics.gov.uk in the United Kingdom, and http://www.census.gov in the United States.
■ **Attitudes or behaviours:** People may share opinions about specific topics (e.g., opposed to nuclear power), or actions they may (or may not) take (e.g., cycling to work). Within the United Kingdom, broad attitudinal groups have been identified specifically in relation to science: 'confident', 'sceptical enthusiasts', less confident', 'distrustful' and 'indifferent' (*Public Attitudes to Science 2008*, published by Research Councils UK and the Department for Innovation, Universities and Skills). Similar groups have been identified within Europe (using the Eurobarometer survey) and America (through the 2006 Science and Engineering indicators research by the National Science Foundation).
■ **Interests:** A group of like-minded people who share a common interest, for example sports teams, social groups, hobbies or community organizations such as Rotary Clubs and the Women's Institute.

Audience targeting

Once the key characteristics of an audience have been identified it is much easier to determine what might interest them or how they might best be engaged in the activity. For example, if you know their educational background the content and language can be tailored to an appropriate level. Or if you are trying to target a specific subgroup (e.g., one particular gender or ethnicity) then you can use examples, role models and case studies that are relevant to that subgroup.

Understanding audience characteristics will also assist in identifying possible 'hooks' to draw the audience into the activity. This is best achieved through direct consultation with representatives of the target audience – especially if you and your project team are not from the same demographic, attitudinal or interest group. They will be able to give their opinions directly, so that the project team doesn't have to second-guess their interests.

Targeting an audience according to their existing interests can be particularly effective: the group members are already in the habit of meeting, have a common interest and purpose, and are likely to feel comfortable and at ease within the existing group environment. These factors immediately increase their receptiveness and ability to engage – the trick then is to make the science relevant and accessible to them. One of the best models for reaching an interest group is to go directly to them: travel to their environment rather than expect them to proactively visit a scientific event, activity or organization. This can be done either formally, for example addressing a meeting, or informally, for example by running a relevant activity in a location where the interest group are likely to be – such as an interactive and entertaining activity about physics for teenagers in a skate park. These *generic venues* can prove extremely successful at engaging an audience. Further advice about running such events is available within the *Physics to Go!* pack: http://www.einsteinyear.org/get_involved/physicstogo/. See Box 6.1 for a case study of how Einstein was taken to Glastonbury.

BOX 6.1   CASE STUDY: *EINSTEIN AT GLASTONBURY*

Young adults (aged between say 18 and 30) are one of the most difficult audiences to access for science communication. School-aged students are a relatively easy 'captive' audience; it is easy to identify where they are and how to reach them. Similarly, older adults tend to have a stronger connection with societal institutions, and may be reached directly through museums, lectures, debates and science cafes, or indirectly through projects that are primarily aimed at their children and/or grandchildren. However institutions such as museums suffer a major deficit in the 18–30 year old age bracket. How do we reach those young people who are not naturally inclined towards science? The answer is to take science directly to them in a manner that they find appealing yet quirky, in surroundings that they have personally chosen, and an environment in which they feel relaxed and yet open to new ideas. Music festivals are one such environment that has been used successfully to reach this audience.

Einstein at Glastonbury involved taking physics demonstrations to one of the UK's most well-known music festivals – Glastonbury Festival of Contemporary Performing Arts. A dynamic team of young science communicators delivered enthusiastic and oftentimes impromptu demonstrations, educating and entertaining the crowd with a variety of physics-based tricks. In homage to the theme of the festival, several of the demonstrations were music related, including the creation of musical instruments from everyday materials, such as coat-hangers and paper cups. As outlined in the final report for the event, *Einstein at Glastonbury* was extremely successful:

The levels of engagement experienced by participants were the highest observed by any of the team members at a public performance event. Audience reactions to the stall were extremely positive. Around 1,500 festival-goers were made directly aware of Einstein Year, and over 500 individuals participated in demonstrations and discussions with the performers.

On the face of it, few music festival attendees would initially be interested in discussing scientific concepts. However, by carefully targeting the audience and understanding their interests, concerns and motivations, the project successfully engaged an otherwise difficult-to-reach cohort with physics. This audience targeting was achieved through taking the physics demonstrations *to* the festival-goers (i.e., targeting the audience directly), ensuring they were fun and entertaining and in keeping with the open-minded mentality of the festival surroundings, and delivered by young people (peers of the target audience). Whilst this exact approach is unlikely to work at every music concert or festival, by carefully adapting the event to suit Glastonbury Festival, this activity succeeded in engaging a normally very hard-to-reach audience.

Methods of direct communication

There are a wide variety of methods that are used to communicate science directly to public audiences, the most obvious of which are public lectures and practical workshops. This section briefly outlines the key features of the most prominent methods of direct communication. Note that a wide variety of methods are possible; priority has been given to the most commonly used methods as well as to providing an idea of the contrasting opportunities that are available.

Public lectures

Lectures are the most traditional form of science communication, harking back to Michael Faraday and the Royal Institution of Great Britain in the 1820s. A presenter provides a description of their research, usually supported by a computer presentation and live demonstrations. This type of intervention can be made more audience interactive through encouraging audience discussion and questions throughout, or even a choose-your-own-lecture format which gives the audience ownership of which aspects (from a specified selection) they would like to hear about.

Practical workshops

Workshops involve the participants in actively designing and/or building something, usually with advice and assistance from a communicator. At many science centres and museums family groups participate in 'make and take' workshops where participants build something they can take away with them.

For example, they might make a mask with moving parts or a small robot based on simple sensors from easily obtained, cheap materials. Workshops often work best when organized in partnership with an existing venue or event, which will recruit the audience and take care of the logistics. Scientists interested in communicating their research now have plentiful opportunities to run workshops (either scheduled or drop-in) at events such as Science Festivals.

Science fairs

Usually held for school students, a Science Fair is a competition where participants develop a small exhibit demonstrating a particular scientific principle, for example how volcanoes work or magnetic properties of different materials. The exhibits are then displayed in a large hall which families and other students are invited to visit. The judging criteria cover both the scientific demonstration as well as the student's ability to describe and explain their exhibit. Some larger scale Fairs encourage participants to perform original research. Winners from national competitions may be nominated for the Intel International Science and Engineering Fair, the world's largest international pre-college science competition which annually provides a forum for more than 1,500 high school students from over 40 countries to showcase their independent research.

Cafés scientifique

Participants are given the opportunity to delve into the latest scientific developments in an informal atmosphere. There is usually an advertised speaker (for example a local academic researcher) who introduces the topic and provides some background (usually up to 15 minutes in total); however the focus of the event is very much on audience discussion. Described by a variety of names in different parts of the world (for example, sci bars, café sci etc.), cafés scientifique have a common focus in that meetings take place in informal contexts – cafés or bars – that are outside a traditional academic environment. Although cafés scientifique were originally started as a way of recruiting young *adults* to debate scientific issues, a Junior Café Scientifique movement (amongst school students) has also arisen. See http://www.cafescientifique.org or http://www.cafe-sci.org.uk/jun.html for further details, including how to set up your own café scientifique.

Science theatre

Scientists and theatre professionals can collaborate to produce a unique perspective on a scientific topic, or raise public interest in a particular issue. For example Michael Frayn's award winning play *Copenhagen* considers a controversial historical encounter between physicists Werner Heisenberg and Neils Bohr. Both dramatists and science communicators tend to see such activities as an opportunity to attract new audiences not normally in contact with their work. The plays may be performed in a normal theatre environment or adapted to visit external venues, for example schools, museums, festivals and so on.

Comparison of methods of direct communication

The various methods of directly communicating with an audience all have their respective pros and cons. Consideration of which aspects are most important for a particular audience and event will help you determine which method to use. For this purpose, Table 6.2 summarizes the main features of each communication method, including indications of typical audience size, the cost incurred and the resources required (both time and consumables). An indication of the 'impact' is also provided, referring to how deeply the average participant gets involved in the activity.

Table 6.2 Comparative features of different types of direct communication methods. All data are specified *per event.*

Communication method	Audience size[#]	Cost[*]	Time required[§]	Equipment required[†]	Impact[‡]
Public lectures	up to 200	~£200	~5 hours	props, microphone?	1 hour; passive
Practical workshops	up to 20	~£40	~ 2 hours	glue, simple tools, cheap consumables	~½ hour; interactive
Science fairs	~100	~£500	~2 weeks	tables, poster boards, exhibits	~1 hour; interactive
Cafés scientifique	up to 30	~£40	~3 hours	minimal	~2 hours; interactive
Science theatre	potentially hundreds	£1,000+	months	theatre / performance space, actors etc.	~2 hours; passive

Notes:

[#] Data specified are for *typical* audience sizes; individual examples may vary.

[*] Up-front costs common to all communication methods are venue and equipment hire, and transport and subsistence of speakers and/or participants.

[§] The time required includes both preparation and delivery time.

[†] The most common equipment is listed.

[‡] The impact column indicates how long (on average) the audience participants are involved as well as the nature of their involvement. 'Passive' indicates that the majority of the participants won't interact with the communicator; 'interactive' indicates a strong hands-on element although relatively short-lived.

From Table 6.2 it is clear that activities which have a high impact (i.e., tend towards 'interactive' rather than 'passive') tend to be ones that are only able to reach a small audience. This makes sense; low audience numbers mean each individual is more heavily involved in the activity, and therefore more likely to benefit from the intervention. However it does mean that there is a compromise to be made between how many people an event can reach, and what level of impact it is likely to have on them. This is an important factor to keep in mind when deciding what sort of event is most appropriate for your purpose.

BOX 6.2   CASE STUDY: THE *SHELL QUESTACON SCIENCE CIRCUS*

In some cases it is advantageous to combine different types of complementary communication methods – in this way the overall programme has far more impact than any of the activities would alone. The Shell Questacon Science Circus is one such example of a very successful long-term programme containing a wide range of activities. The Circus tours Australia for 18–20 weeks each year bringing lively presentations of science to towns and schools throughout Australia.

The Science Circus consists of

- a travelling exhibition containing 50 hands-on science exhibits
- interesting and entertaining science shows performed for both school and public audiences
- teacher notes and resources for each of the school shows
- practical and fun professional development workshops for teachers

The travel costs associated with the Science Circus are significant, and in many similar situations would be considered prohibitive. However there are two key advantages to Questacon's approach in this matter. Firstly, by including activities for both students and teachers the team achieves much more than would be possible with only a single target audience. Secondly, by focusing on rural and regional communities the Science Circus is able to reach people who wouldn't otherwise be able to engage with these sorts of activities, since their communities are located too far from any of the science centres or museums within Australia (which are generally located within the larger cities).

In addition, by contributing a variety of different activity types (e.g., both hands-on exhibits and demonstration lectures) the Science Circus can maximize the impact of their activities and appeal to different audiences.

The impact of the Shell Questacon Science Circus is therefore greatly enhanced through both the provision of multiple complementary activities and by specifically targeting new audiences.

Planning and preparation

Adequate planning and preparation is essential for successful communication. This section describes both general principles behind preparing to communicate science directly to an audience, as well as key questions to ask during this process.

The fundamental principle behind planning and preparing an activity is to make sure it is tailored specifically to the audience and environment you will encounter. As outlined previously in this chapter, audience needs differ greatly, and an activity which is designed for one audience will almost certainly not transfer effectively to another. Poor communicators rehash their materials; effective communicators adapt to each and every scenario. This does not have to be an overly onerous task, for example the same images and videos might be appropriate to different age groups, so long as the language and complexity of the ideas is adjusted accordingly. The key is to consider the audience and their needs in advance, and adjust your presentation accordingly.

Tips for effective preparation

- **Define key messages/aims/learning outcomes:** what is it that you hope to achieve through the activity? If necessary, write it down in advance. The process of defining these aspects will clarify your thoughts and help to focus the presentation. Limit the number of messages you plan to deliver, and make sure they are aligned to the event aims.
- **Have a plan ...:** Detail in advance how you propose to run the activity, including timings, responsibilities, resources etc. Review this plan critically. Have you forgotten anything? Will it fit within the time/space available (including setup/packup)? Do you have all the resources needed? What is likely to go wrong and do you have a backup option? If anything seems unfeasible it is better to know in advance, and adjust your plan accordingly.
- **...and stick to it!:** Once you have a plan you are happy with, use it! Make sure everyone involved in the activity is aware of the plan and understands their role within it. Keep an eye on the time during the activity; if anything isn't working or is running behind then can it be adapted and still achieve your aims?
- **Play to your strengths:** You will appear more relaxed, confident and enthusiastic if you are speaking about a topic you are knowledgeable and enthusiastic about. Also consider your other strengths – for example, can you sing, act or draw? Are you able to describe complex ideas using simple analogies? In areas where you feel you are weak, do you have any colleagues who could help? You don't have to do everything yourself, and the activity will benefit from other people's complementary input.
- **Be confident but not over-ambitious:** Be realistic in what you set out to achieve. It might be a wonderful activity that really engages the audience; however, it is unlikely to create an overnight stampede of applications to science degrees at the local university.
- **Do your homework:** Find out as much information as possible in advance. Key questions to ask include:

1. Who is the audience? What are their ages, backgrounds etc.? Do they know one another? What is their motivation for attending? (see the section on Catering for different audiences.)

2. How long am I speaking for? Who else is involved and what are they doing?
3. What is the purpose of the session?
4. What are the logistical arrangements? What is/isn't allowed within the venue? What parking/time constraints are there? How long do I have for setup and pack-up? Who is paying for my travel/time (if appropriate)?

By keeping the above points in mind you will be able to identify potential problems in advance, and produce an event that is well suited to the audience, subject matter and venue. Of course things might still go wrong, however by having thought about it thoroughly in advance you will be much more familiar with potential solutions, so more able to adapt to crises.

Presentation and facilitation skills

Science communicators take on a range of different roles when they interact with audiences. For example they might present a lecture or show to a large audience, or answer questions in an informal environment, or even facilitate a discussion amongst groups of varying sizes. Communication skills are key in all of these scenarios. This section provides advice on how to develop skills in presentation and facilitation.

Note that both aspects are equally important. When presenting a lecture it is still crucial that you are able to facilitate Q&A sessions with the audience, whilst in smaller groups it is important to both present information and facilitate the discussions with equal ease.

The only way to develop these skills effectively is through practice and critical feedback. Where possible, try to get a recording of yourself in action, or get someone you trust to give feedback on your abilities. Very few people enjoy watching themselves on video, however it will provide a real insight into how you interact with the audience.

Presentation skills

Good presentation skills are crucial if you are to communicate your ideas successfully. In general, you should:

- Do your research beforehand
- Know your audience
- Practise in front of a mirror/friend, and in the venue where possible
- Use a crib sheet if you think it helps
- Don't read
- Enjoy yourself (but you should always feel nervous!)

Tables 6.3 to 6.6 provide examples of good and bad practice for a variety of different presentation skills, as well as specific advice on methods of improving those skills.

Table 6.3 Examples of good and bad practice and advice for improving general communication skills

General	Good practice	Poor practice	Advice
Effective start	Clear introduction including name and topic. Wait for silence.	Launching straight in, not waiting for audience to stop talking, no name.	Let the audience know you are ready to begin by standing still and looking around the room, or if necessary calling their attention.
Appearance	Appropriate for the audience. Visible against the background.	Scruffy or overly smart. Wearing white when presenting against a white background. Distracting clothing.	Think about how you come across from the audience's point of view, and how you want to be perceived.
Health and safety	Completing a risk assessment, and adhering to it. Being aware of and reacting to unexpected events.	Doing anything that puts the audience at risk.	You can do all sorts of things, just make sure you have completed a risk assessment. Take particular care where children are involved both for your and their safety.
Habitual twitches	Natural movements without noticeable regular twitches (vocal or physical).	Being unaware of that itchy knee you've suddenly developed, or saying 'um' a lot.	Watch yourself on video, or get someone you trust to tell you what bad speaking habits you have.
Gestures	Complete and useful gestures.	Incomplete, unnecessary gestures that are distracting.	As with habitual twitches, find out what you do. Always use complete gestures. You are not trying to become wooden and eliminate your personality; let your personality shine through.
Visibility on stage	Standing where you can see all your audience.	Skulking in a corner.	If you can see your audience, they can see you.

Continued

Table 6.3 Continued

General	Good practice	Poor practice	Advice
Accuracy of content	Do your research.	Lying.	Don't make unsubstantiated claims; admit if you don't know something.
Effective end	Summarize, end with something memorable and relevant. Clear ending.	Tailing off, rushing to include everything.	Practice your ending; be sure about what your final words will be and speak confidently and clearly right to the last word.
Time of presentation	Stick to time, or just less than time.	Do not overrun, ever.	If you have been given 5 minutes, then talk for 5 minutes (or less if you need to include questions). Keep an eye on the time as you go. Rehearse so you know the timings.

Table 6.4 Examples of good and bad practice and advice for improving speaking skills

Speaking	Good practice	Poor practice	Advice
Voice speed	Well paced, but with some variation.	Speaking very quickly or stumbling over your words.	Practise, record yourself. When you are speaking, if you think you are speaking too slowly you are probably speaking at about the right speed.
Voice volume	Clearly heard throughout the room.	Too quiet (most common) or shouting.	Use vocal exercises to warm up in advance; have water to hand; open your mouth.
Language used	Language used reflects that of the audience.	Overly complex or simplistic language; use of jargon without explanations.	Know the audience and the language they will be used to. Asking questions at the beginning is a useful way of finding this out. Adopt their own words where possible.
Narrative/ flow	Well structured and logical.	Jumps around, no flow, no beginning, middle or end.	Make sure you have some sort of narrative – it is easier to remember and the audience can follow it too.

Table 6.5   Examples of good and bad practice and advice for improving skills in interacting with the audience

Interacting with the audience	Good practice	Poor practice	Advice
Making eye contact	Everyone receives some eye contact from you.	Not looking at anyone, or focusing on only one person.	It is important that the audience feel you are talking to them, do this by looking at them all (or appearing to!). Spectacles can hinder eye contact; be aware of this and compensate.
Asking questions	Questions are relevant to the topic and the audience, are clearly worded. No rhetorical questions unless clearly intended.	Audience are asked questions but not given a chance to answer them. No questions asked. Questions are too difficult or too simple for the audience.	Questions to the audience are really useful for you and for the audience. Make sure you ask questions that the audience can answer and give them instructions as to how to answer e.g., hands up, shout out.
Answering questions	Using the participant's own phrasing in the response.	Not addressing misconceptions.	There's no point asking questions if you don't answer them. Make the audience feel involved by using their own wording in your explanations.
	Correcting wrong answers tactfully.	Correcting answers with a harsh 'no, that's not right'	When answering audience questions, keep your audience in mind; use analogies and references to previous discussions to reinforce key concepts.
Humour	Jokes are at a level and in a style appropriate for the audience.	Jokes are offensive to the audience or contain language or references that they don't understand.	Use humour to get the audience on your side, but make sure it is appropriate. If your jokes are falling flat – stop and play it straight.
		No humour used.	Obviously, be careful of using humour when talking about a delicate matter, but don't dismiss it out of hand.

Table 6.6 Examples of good and bad practice and advice for using equipment

Use of equipment	Good practice	Poor practice	Advice
Choice of equipment	Used appropriately and only when necessary, e.g., computer slides are good for images, defining terms, video; flip charts for gathering audience inputs.	Directly reading the slide text. Inappropriate formatting, e.g., too much text, crazy colours, distracting animations, illegible, spelling mistakes...	Choose equipment carefully: what purpose will it serve; will it enhance or detract from what you are saying? Keep any slides used clear and simple; test them out on a large screen in advance. Practice writing on a flip chart to determine the minimum writing size for the room dimensions.
Use of equipment	Equipment helps to move the presentation along. This could be a demonstration or just using the AV appropriately.	Having something to show that isn't relevant. Using AV equipment that is inappropriate. Having unreliable equipment.	Equipment of any kind must be reliable and you must have practised with it, in the venue. Make sure it is the correct size for the venue.
Confidence with equipment	Well rehearsed and confident with equipment.	Not practised with the equipment, fumbling.	Don't have demonstrations for the sake of it, but equally, a good demo can speak a thousand words.

Facilitation skills

A facilitator's role is to provide all participants with an opportunity to be involved in a discussion, to share their ideas and opinions, and to feel comfortable whilst doing so.

Why encourage discussion? The primary reason is to encourage the audience to become active participants in the activity. Additional benefits include providing participants with an opportunity to:

- evaluate theories
- synthesize approaches
- develop new interests
- find out what they (and others) do or do not believe
- gain confidence in their intellectual abilities
- question and think about a topic in more depth
- help them learn how to learn

There is a wide range of training courses, books and websites providing specific advice on facilitation skills for various circumstances, however the following common aspects apply:

- **Welcome:** It is important that all participants feel comfortable and understand the scope of the activity. If possible, introduce yourself to each participant as they arrive, or do so as a group.
- **Ground rules:** Agree at the start how the group will operate, for example, how questions will be asked/answered, that all opinions are equally respected etc. If time permits it is usually best if the participants as a group agree on these ground rules at the start.
- **Neutrality:** The facilitator should demonstrate neutrality towards the topic under discussion; it is sometimes preferable to bring in an external facilitator for particularly controversial or emotive issues.
- **Probing and prompting, not talking:** The facilitator should seek to obtain the group's opinions and ideas, rather than outline his/her own thoughts. Phrase your questions neutrally and encourage participants to elaborate their reasons, rather than just a short answer. Prepare in advance some 'killer facts' to drop into the conversation to trigger reactions from the audience, and include alternative opinions or suggestions as to what other people might say (this is particularly useful in the case of homogenous groups).
- **Seating:** Arrange the chairs so that all participants have a good view of each other (and the facilitator). For larger groups it is useful for the facilitator to be able to move around between participants, so allow space for this.
- **Clear directions:** Clearly signal who will speak next, and during the discussions be aware of people who are interested in contributing. If they catch your eye then give them a small nod to indicate that you've seen their interest, then allow them to speak next in turn. Don't allow people to interrupt or talk over other participants, and try to encourage all participants to be involved.
- **Plan ahead:** Have a clear plan of what you want to achieve, and plan some interactive activities ahead of time that will get the whole group involved in case discussion dries up. For example, ranking exercises can be used to identify the group's priorities about a topic, or simple voting sessions where participants raise their hands to indicate their opinions on a specific issue.
- **Keep focused:** Summarize and organize participant's responses to draw together common threads; keep the question or issue under consideration in view at all times.

Common fears

It is natural to be concerned about giving a presentation or facilitating an important meeting, and in fact many professionals agree that a degree of nervousness is necessary for a good performance. The most frequent worry is that something will go wrong and the performance or activity won't be perfect. This is just a fact of life – it is almost certain that something will go wrong. No-one is faultless, however if you have prepared thoroughly and can respond calmly then the audience won't even notice that something untoward has occurred.

Some presenters get concerned that they don't know what to say, or won't be able to answer the questions. In this case, remember that you have been asked to be involved for a reason – someone recognizes your expertise, and that you are the right person to be doing this task. Have your opening and closing sentences ready and thoroughly rehearsed – this will prevent you from 'freezing' at the start, and ensure you end with a bang. When answering questions try to keep responses short – these should be limited to one or two key points (sentences) per question – and if you don't know the answer to a question, admit it. The audience will be able to tell if you are making something up, and will respect you more if you respond with something along the lines of 'That's a very interesting question, I'd like to know the answer to that myself – I'll find out and let you (or the teacher or organizer) know after the show'. If you think someone in the audience may know the answer then you could even invite the audience to respond to the question instead.

Finally, many people get concerned about saying something stupid and being laughed at or not listened to. If you make a small mistake then it really doesn't matter – people will take away the important part, and you could use humour to acknowledge mistakes. If you have prepared properly and know your audience then they will be on your side, or – in the case of antagonistic and disruptive audience members – it is well within your rights to ask those people to move or leave if they are really causing a problem. You are there to communicate your science, not to act as a disciplinarian, therefore make use of teachers/carers/event organizers if necessary.

Creating resources

Almost every science communication activity will require some sort of resources to be produced: simple flyers may be needed for advertising, while posters and slides may be shown during the actual intervention. More complex resources such as packs and manuals for the participants involved may also be needed. Developing these resources takes time and effort and can be costly. Here are some tips to help ensure these resources are effective:

■ **Utilize your skills...:** Do you have a particular skill that could help make the resources stand out? Are you good at drawing, or coming up with jokes and puns, or different computer packages? If so then take advantage of these skills when developing your resources.
■ **...and those of your colleagues/acquaintances/friends:** If you don't have a particular skill yourself, ask around – someone else might. If it doesn't

take too much time then many people will be happy to help you out, either by drawing graphics, writing the publicity text, designing your slide background or even distributing the flyers for you.

- **Where possible, go professional:** particularly for prestigious and/or important events, consider involving professionals. This could range from expert facilitators to event managers, media experts, even exhibit fabricators. If you work at an organization with a press or PR department, or an outreach centre, or a graphic design office, or whatever other professional skills that might be relevant, then make use of them.

- **Obtain input and/or feedback:** regardless of the size of the event, it is important to get feedback on the resources. This could range from having a colleague look over the slides, to speaking to representatives from the target audience to see if the ideas are adequately tailored to them (see the section on Catering for different audiences in this chapter).

- **Consider audience needs:** Make sure the content is appropriate to the audience; adjust images, text, case studies, examples and vocabulary as appropriate. Keep in mind aspects such as colour blindness – so don't display graphs with a red and a green line for comparison (or other inappropriate combinations). Also consider different learning styles: use a mixture of delivery styles including text, graphics, video or oral descriptions and analogies and case studies.

- **Clear and aesthetically pleasing:** Use a simple and easy-to-read font, and ensure that any printed material has an obvious path for the reader to follow. Use graphics and images as well as text (see below the section on Learning styles). Use colours to highlight and enhance, not detract from the resource. Make sure the overall size is appropriate: print out or project a test version of the resource well in advance, and stand where the audience are likely to be so you can see it from their perspective.

- **Careful editing:** Keep text clear and concise, and avoid using jargon. Use short sentences and explain any abbreviations. Use spellcheckers and/or grammar references if necessary.

- **Is PowerPoint necessary?:** Most presentations now rely on using PowerPoint slides or their equivalent; however presenters often read from it verbatim rather than using it as a tool to highlight key points. Consider in advance whether it is in fact necessary to use slides, and if so then keep them to a minimum.

Learning styles

It is widely recognized that different people learn in different ways. Some people respond better to visual prompts (e.g., a diagram or map to find their way) whilst others prefer to use text (e.g., a list of directions). It is important to take these different learning styles into account when planning an event: it is highly likely that there will be people with different learning preferences present. According to http://www.vark-learn.com there are four commonly recognized learning styles:

- **Visual:** Learners benefit from the representation of information in graphical form rather than text, for example maps, charts, graphs and flow charts. However animated representations such as movies and videos or text-based PowerPoint slides do *not* come under a 'visual' learning style.
- **Aural:** Learners prefer information that is 'heard or spoken'; being verbally told or discussing ideas. This can include talking out loud as well as talking to yourself.
- **Read/write:** Learners prefer information displayed as text; reading and writing in all its forms.
- **Kinaesthetic:** Learners prefer the use of experience and practice, whether it be simulated or real. For example, they learn best from demonstrations, simulations, videos and movies of 'real' things, as well as case studies, practice and applications.

What this means is that each activity or output that you prepare should be checked to ensure that it caters for all four learning styles. Using a variety of styles (e.g., text interspersed with images and case studies) will also maintain the audience's interest and keep them engaged and motivated.

Dos and don'ts of live experiments and demonstrations

In showbiz there is the old adage 'never work with children or animals'. Perhaps 'live demonstrations' should also be included; it often seems that whatever *can* possibly go wrong in a demonstration lecture *will* go wrong. However demonstrations can also make the difference between a boring lecture and an inspirational experience. This section describes the key Dos and Don'ts of performing science experiments in public.

Practice and planning

As is highlighted elsewhere in this chapter, planning is paramount to a successful performance. The demonstration should form an integral part of the performance, not be 'tagged on', so make sure the descriptions before and afterwards refer naturally to the demonstration.

For live demonstrations it is particularly important to practice the experiment repeatedly, so that the demonstration is performed smoothly and with the minimum of fuss. Frequent practising will also identify what problems might arise with the demonstration – and how they can be overcome if necessary!

Rehearse explanations whilst doing the demonstration – this will help you determine where you should stand to perform it, as well as how detailed the explanation needs to be to cover the length of time it takes to do the demonstration. Keep the explanation clear and concise, using the demonstration to highlight key points.

Keep a list of the equipment required for each demonstration, and check in advance that it is all ready and waiting. Many performers find it easier if they set up all their equipment in the order that they will use it – this will not only highlight if something is missing, but also remind them what comes next should they forget!

Technical equipment

If using specialist equipment then make sure you leave plenty of time to set it up (and pack it up again after the performance). Again, making sure you know exactly how to operate it (especially if something goes wrong) is crucial for maintaining the audience's interest and confidence in you.

If buying new equipment then test it thoroughly – if it is particularly expensive then ask to see a demonstration of the equipment in action in advance. In particular, make sure the test occurs in exactly the same circumstances as it will operate within the performance, for example an electronic voting system might work well in a small room with a limited number of handsets, however fail in a large lecture hall.

Consider whether you need to use a microphone, and if so then test it out in advance, and have it ready before the audience arrives. If performing live experiments then do *not* use a handheld microphone – you will not be able to hold the microphone and perform the experiments at the same time.

Alternative option

Have a back up plan in case anything goes wrong. This could range from an alternative experiment to an animation or simulation or even an explanation of what *should* have happened. Don't dwell on what went wrong – the audience won't necessarily know what should have happened, and may not even notice that the demonstration failed. Finish the explanation of the current topic then move swiftly on to the next section.

Visibility and design

Make sure demonstrations are designed for the type of venue in which they will be performed. If it's a small room then loud bangs or extremely messy demonstrations may not be appropriate; similarly, in a large hall smaller experiments may not be visible to the majority of the audience. Consider using a video camera projected onto a screen to provide a clear view of what is happening in smaller experiments. Many microscopes now have external outputs, and standard CCTV cameras and webcams can be inexpensive solutions to showing small demonstrations to large audiences.

Using volunteers

Including volunteers in a performance is a great way of increasing audience interaction. Choose volunteers appropriately: make sure they are the right age/size/maturity etc. to provide assistance for the demonstration. Give them clear instructions throughout their involvement and make them feel welcome – ask their name and introduce them to the audience. *Never* make fun of volunteers, or put them in a position where they feel uncomfortable or unsafe. Don't leave them standing around with nothing to do either; if an experiment takes a long time, then ask them to come back at a later stage of the performance. Thank them when they have completed their task and ask the audience to give them a round of applause.

Health and safety

In this day and age health and safety considerations are paramount: lecturers, venues and teachers all need to complete rigorous risk assessments, and many schools are no longer able to perform certain demonstrations in the classroom due to fears of safety for the students should anything go wrong. This should not put you off; with appropriate precautions and forward planning almost any demonstration is feasible. Treat safety seriously: do a thorough risk assessment, get it checked by an appropriate safety officer (either within your institution or the venue), and stick to the specified mitigation measures. It's also worth looking into the insurance situation: if your institution's policy doesn't cover you for the proposed activities then consider taking out personal liability insurance – many large venues won't accept your performance without it.

Most institutions will have their own safety guidelines and advice in place; however it is also worth investigating the guidance provided by national teaching networks and advisory groups regarding appropriate health and safety procedures. Although specific to a school environment, they tend to be relatively straightforward and may be easily adapted to more general public locations.

Sourcing experiments

Live experiments have been performed in public for many years, and cover a wide variety of science topics, venue types and audience sizes. In all likelihood someone has either already performed the experiment you wish to use, or has tried it previously and abandoned the attempt because it didn't work or wasn't effective. Learn from this – there's no point in reinventing the wheel. With the advent of the Internet it is even easier to access resources and information about existing experiments; a selection of the best is provided below.

- British Interactive Group: http://www.big.uk.com, has advice and ideas for anything interactive; also has an associated mailing list (BIG-chat) which is very informal and where members are only too happy to share their experiences and ideas.

- The Exploratorium: http://www.exploratorium.edu
- Krampf Experiment of the Week: http://www.krampf.com/news.html
- Little Book of Experiments by Planet Science: http://www.planet-science. com/sciteach/index.html?page=/experiment/
- The Naked Scientists Kitchen Science Experiments: http://www. thenakedscientists.com/HTML/content/kitchenscience/
- Physics to Go!: http://www.einsteinyear.org/get_involved/physicstogo/
- Planet Scicast: http://www.planet-scicast.com/
- Planet Science's Wired Science Magic Box: http://www.scienceyear.com/ wired/index.html?page=/wired/magicbox
- Professor Shakhashiri: http://www.scifun.chem.wisc.edu
- SciZmic, the Science Discovery Clubs network: http://www.scizmic.net
- Simple Science from science made simple: http://www.sciencemadesimple. co.uk/page28g.html
- Steve Spangler Science: http://www.stevespanglerscience.com/experiments
- The Surfing Scientist by the Australian Broadcasting Corporation: http:// www.abc.net.au/science/surfingscientist/

Reflection and evaluation

Good presenters are constantly improving their performance, adapting their activities to better suit their audience, and integrating new developments and opportunities. This section describes how to reflect effectively upon and evaluate your activity, including brief explanations of different techniques and when they are appropriate.

There are excellent existing guides available on evaluating science communication projects; two of the best are:

- RCUK's Evaluation: Practical Guidelines: http://www.rcuk.ac.uk/news/ evaluation.htm
- Ingenious Evaluation Toolkit: http://www.raeng.org.uk/about/engagement/ evaluation.htm

Why reflect and evaluate?

There are a variety of reasons why it is important to reflect upon activities and/ or evaluate them, including to

- Identify if the aims/objectives have been met
- Identify if unintended outcomes have occurred
- Publicize personal achievements and learn from mistakes

■ Provide evidence to enable the activities to be continued (e.g., for funding bodies, line managers and institutions)

■ Learn from the experience and improve the activities in the future

Evaluation techniques

Evaluation is most effective when it is performed not only at the end of a project (*summative* evaluation) but also during a project (*formative* evaluation). Reflection on the management and operation of the project is known as *process* evaluation, and should also occur during the project development. Both quantitative and qualitative techniques are used to evaluate projects.

The main technique for recording self-reflections is a *thought diary*. The presenter will usually have their own gut feeling as to how an activity has gone, and their perspective can be invaluable for determining what worked and what didn't work in an event. Thought diaries are usually completed by members of the project team, and can be either formalized (e.g., an entry is made after each and every activity) or informal (reflections occur whenever an important issue or idea arises).

Self-reflection can allow you to identify personal strengths and weaknesses, and how to improve your performance; however it is also important to get regular feedback from other people to ensure that you are heading in the right direction. The following are possible methods of obtaining feedback directly from participants:

■ **Questionnaires:** Questionnaires are one of the simplest evaluation methods to use, and often allows a large sample size to be obtained. Questionnaires may be distributed either in hardcopy or online, and outline a series of specific questions which participants are asked to answer. The questions may be *closed* (where participants choose from a range of pre-selected responses) or *open* (where participants are free to provide any answer that occurs to them). Online questionnaires have the advantage of not requiring the data to be entered into a computer for analysis, however may preclude certain people from responding, for example because their computer system won't accept the site or software (e.g., some schools have stringent firewalls), or because the participant doesn't have access to a computer at the appropriate time.

■ **Interviews and focus groups:** The primary methods of obtaining qualitative data are through interviews and focus groups. Although the sample sizes are generally much smaller (due to the longer time taken for the discussion itself as well as transcription, analysis and so on), both interviews and focus groups enable a much deeper look at a topic or issue, and provide more freedom to investigate the reasoning behind a participant's views. It is common for interviews and focus groups to be used during the development stages of a project, with the results being used to formulate a questionnaire for use in later stages.

■ **Observations:** Direct observation of the audience can provide a variety of subtle information about their reaction to the activity. Their body language, facial expressions, interest in asking or answering questions etc. can all provide subconscious indicators as to how engaged the audience are in the activity. Observation methods can range from an unobtrusive observer writing down their impressions of audience reactions (usually according to a pre-determined observation schedule) to recording a video of the audience throughout the event.

In addition to the above standard techniques, a variety of more creative methods have been devised in order to best suit specific performances and events. For example, live feedback can be obtained via SMS messaging to a given number, or participants can leave their thoughts and suggestions on a 'graffiti wall' near an exhibit. In the case of a physically interactive event it might be appropriate to have the participants represent their response to a particular question by physically standing along a scale across one side of the room. The standard techniques above can also be adapted to encompass more creative aspects; for example the interviews might be delivered by peers instead of the researcher (which may produce more honest responses), or simple questionnaires could be delivered on postcards or folded into paper planes, with a competition as to who could get theirs in the collection box.

Ethical considerations

It is important to note that since all of the above are concerned with asking participants their personal opinions, ethical issues arise such as confidentiality and anonymity of information. This is particularly the case when working with children and other groups perceived as vulnerable. Most institutions will have internal guidelines designed to ensure such research is performed ethically. General guidelines are provided by professional market research organizations, such as MRS in the United Kingdom and the Australian Market and Social Research Society (http://www.mrs.org.uk/standards/guidelines.htm and http://www.mrsa.com.au/respectively).

Potential drawbacks to direct communication methods

The major difficulty in becoming involved in communicating science to public audiences is the time and resources required to do so. Many people find it difficult to fit in amongst their other priorities, and in particular, senior staff may question its importance compared to their staff's regular 'day job'. Arguably, this is a short-term view which ignores the downward trend in pupils selecting science subjects at school and university within western countries – without appropriate engagement and recruitment of future scientists and engineers there will be no-one with the appropriate skills to do that day job in the future. This attitude is gradually changing, especially in the United Kingdom with strong government support and the development of the Beacons for Public Engagement (see http://www.publicengagement.ac.uk/default.htm).

Occasionally an event or activity may appear to be unappreciated, either by the audience directly or by event organizers. If this is the case, firstly consider whether there was something wrong with the activity or presentation – was it appropriate for the target audience; could it have been improved in any way? Speak to the event organizers and members of the audience where possible – it is feasible that in truth they did appreciate your efforts; however they were not proactive in expressing their thanks. Finally, if your services were taken for granted then find another arena in which to operate – if your efforts are not appreciated then there are plenty of other opportunities available.

Finally, presenters can be thoroughly discouraged when things go wrong. A demonstration might not have worked as you had planned, or an audience might have been disruptive and inattentive, you didn't achieve what you had hoped, or you might just have had a bad day. In all these cases it is worth considering the positive aspects as well as the negative ones. Remember the look of excitement on a child's face when things did go right, and keep in mind that everyone has bad days at times. There was a reason you got involved in communicating science to the public – remember that reason and stick with it! The rewards will outweigh the difficulties eventually.

ACTIVITIES

■ What types of science do you find interesting and why? Cataloguing your interests in science will help you identify which areas you are most comfortable explaining to other people. Thinking about the 'why' question will help you develop angles which you could pursue.

■ Develop a short presentation explaining your favourite scientific concept. Test it out on a friend or a small local audience. If possible, set up a video camera to film you and then review the video, identifying your personal strengths and weaknesses.

■ Think of a practical demonstration, for example a fizzy rocket (made by placing an effervescent tablet and a small amount of water inside a plastic film canister). Practice explaining the demonstration to different audiences, for example a class of seven-year olds? A small group of ten-year olds? An individual 16-year old? A science teacher or professor? What aspects of the explanation remain the same and what aspects differ for the different audiences?

Acknowledgements

The author gratefully acknowledges the assistance and input from the following individuals and institutions in producing this chapter: Clare Wilkinson, Helen Featherstone and Emma Weitkamp from the Science Communication Unit at the University of the West of England; Graham Durant and Questacon, Australia's National Science & Technology Centre; Laura Grant and the Institute of Physics.

References and further reading

The Engineering and Physical Sciences Research Council's Partnerships for Public Awareness Good Practice Guide: http://www.epsrc.ac.uk/CMSWeb/Downloads/Publications/Other/PPA%20Good%20Practice%20Guide.pdf

Fry, H., Ketteridge, S. and Marshall, S. (2002), Understanding Student Learning, in Fry, H. (ed), *Handbook for Teaching and Learning in Higher Education: Enhancing Academic Practice*, Routledge Falmer (London). N.B Although focused on the higher education sector, this chapter contains useful insights into different learning theories, including constructivism, rationalism and situated learning.

Garr Reynolds (2008), *Presentation Zen: Simple Ideas on Presentation Design and Delivery*. New Riders Press (Berkeley).

Rogers, C. (1999), The Importance of Understanding Audiences, in Friedman, S., Dunwoody, S. and Rogers, C. (eds), *Communicating Uncertainty*, Laurence Erlbaum Associates (Mahwah).

Many funding organizations have produced overviews of appropriate evaluation techniques, for example RCUK's Evaluation: Practical Guidelines: http://www.rcuk.ac.uk/news/evaluation.htm.

Communicating Science in Museums and Science Centres

Alison Boyle

7

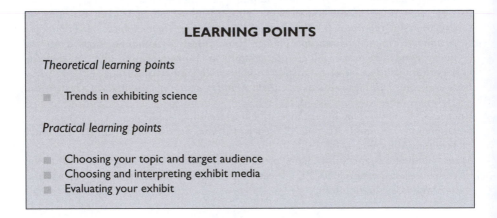

LEARNING POINTS

Theoretical learning points

- Trends in exhibiting science

Practical learning points

- Choosing your topic and target audience
- Choosing and interpreting exhibit media
- Evaluating your exhibit

Introduction

Science museums and science centres combine many of the media explored elsewhere in this book, in addition to an important extra: visitors themselves. Visiting a museum or science centre is an immersive experience which can provide a unique learning opportunity in the context of an enjoyable day out.

'Science' in a museum or hands-on centre often spans many areas: science, technology, engineering, medicine and natural history. Different institutions have different and often complex histories, and different styles of exhibitions.

There are many tasks involved in creating an exhibition. In a large institution your exhibition team could include specialist curators, content developers, designers, technicians, builders, press and marketing officers and hands-on gallery staff. In a small institution you may be doing several, if not all, of these jobs by yourself. Often, there will have to be compromises to ensure that each element of an exhibit is done to the highest possible standard without affecting the quality of other elements. The most important element is of course the content, and that is what this chapter will focus on.

Trends in exhibiting science

Beginnings: curiosity and wonder

Museums have their origins in the Cabinets of Curiosities popular in Europe in the sixteenth and seventeenth centuries. These private collections, ranging in size from specially designed display cupboards to several rooms, would house items of wonder gathered from around the world such as mineral samples, stuffed animals, exotic carvings and unicorn horns (disappointingly for lovers of mythical creatures, these usually turned out to be narwhal tusks). Their owners would painstakingly arrange them according to different classification schemes.

In the United Kingdom, one of the most popular and influential cabinets was 'Tradescant's Ark' in Lambeth, London, collected by John Tradescant and his son of the same name over several decades and catalogued by John the Younger as the *Musaeum Tradescantianum* in 1656. Unlike most cabinets, which could be viewed only by the great and the good on invitation, the Ark was open to any member of the public so long as they paid a small fee. On the younger Tradescant's death the collection passed to Elias Ashmole – despite the protestations of Tradescant's wife, who claimed unsuccessfully that her husband had been drunk when he agreed to hand over the collection by deed. Ashmole later bequeathed the collection, with other items he had amassed, to the University of Oxford. The Ashmolean Museum opened in Oxford in 1683, the world's first purpose-built museum.

The growth of public science museums

The eighteenth and nineteenth centuries saw the setting up of a number of public institutions. The British Museum opened in 1759 (although for some years visits were by appointment only) and the Louvre in 1793. In 1794 the Conservatoire Nationale des Arts et Metiers was founded in Paris to support the development of science and industry. Its museum, housed in a disused abbey, opened in 1802.

The industrial boom of the nineteenth century was reflected in a series of major public exhibitions, which gave rise to some of the world's major science museums. The 1851 Great Exhibition of the Works of Industry of All Nations in Hyde Park showed the best of British art and industry alongside exhibits from around the world. The aim was to inspire British artisans and the exhibition was visited by around 6 million people. The success of the exhibition led to the founding of a government department to encourage science and art and the South Kensington museum. This later split its decorative arts and science collections into the Victoria and Albert Museum and the Science Museum, respectively.

The Great Exhibition was followed by World's Fairs in locations such as Paris (where the Eiffel Tower was built for the 1889 fair), Chicago and San Francisco. In many cases the buildings and some of the exhibits were retained and later became dedicated museums; Chicago Museum of Science and Technology opened in 1933 on the site of the 1893 exhibition.

In the United States, the Smithsonian Institution, founded in 1846, houses the national collections. Its buildings along the Mall in Washington include the National Air and Space Museum (the most visited museum in the world), the National Museum of Natural History, and the National Museum of American History. In Germany, the Deutsches Museum was the brainchild of Oskar von Miller. Open to the public since 1925, its full name translates as the 'German Museum for the masterworks of science and technology'.

In the early days of the museums, the focus was on showcasing new developments in science and industry. There would often be working demonstrations of inventions, and it was common for objects in the collection to be returned to their owners and replaced by the latest models. As the objects in their care became increasingly obsolete, institutions moved away from using their collections to demonstrate existing practices in science and technology, and towards using artefacts to portray the history of science. A different type of institution, the science centre, would take up the mantle of demonstrations.

The rise of the science centre

Hands-on demonstrations are one of the earliest forms of public science communication, as we have seen in Chapter 3. When museums were mainly occupied with displaying the newest inventions it was quite common to have these demonstrated on gallery; however with the move to preserving objects for history the displays have become more static. Also, when you have large numbers of visitors arriving at different times throughout the day, it is difficult to operate with a format that requires a presenter and works best for smaller groups. The solution was to create exhibits with built-in demonstrations, to be operated by visitors themselves.

In 1931 the Science Museum in London opened its Children's Gallery, with exhibits that were designed to be touched and used. In 1969 the Exploratorium opened in San Francisco (see Box 7.1 Case Study), shortly followed by the Ontario Science Centre. Both were designed so that visitors could touch the exhibits and have their curiosity aroused. In the following decades a wide network of science centres has grown across North America.

In the United Kingdom, the Exploratory in Bristol opened in 1979. As the name suggests, it was heavily influenced by its predecessor in San Francisco. There are now more than 100 science centres in the United Kingdom, according to a 2007 Government report. The biggest science centre in Europe is the

Cité des Sciences et de l'Industrie at La Vilette, outside Paris, which opened in 1986. It has been designated as the French national science museum but from the outset it was decided that it would have few objects. It does not have its own collection, but has purchased objects for display.

Meanwhile, many large museums now contain hands-on galleries with exhibits similar to those in science centres. In London, the Science Museum's Children's Gallery gave way to Launch Pad, which first opened in 1984. Twenty-five years on, Launch Pad remains the most popular gallery in the Museum, with two reincarnations in 2000 and 2007. The Deutsches Museum has Kinderreich (Kids' Kingdom) and in Australia, the New South Wales Museum of Applied Arts and Science in Sydney was rebranded in 1988 as the Powerhouse Museum and now combines displays of the museum's historical collection with interactive galleries.

BOX 7.1   CASE STUDY: THE EXPLORATORIUM, SAN FRANCISCO

The Exploratorium is the granddaddy of today's science centres. It was the brain-child of scientist Frank Oppenheimer, inspired by science museums he had visited in Europe. His vision was for science exhibits organized by perception: touch, taste, smell, hearing, vision and movement.

San Francisco – seen as open to new ideas and experimentation – was chosen as the location and the new Exploratorium opened in 1969. Since then it has added many new exhibits and themes. The installations are deliberately designed to look rough-and-ready rather than being attractively slick, encouraging people to use them. Computer-based exhibits are rare, with mechanical exhibits encouraging people to explore phenomena physically rather than by the click of a mouse. Exhibits covering the same topic are grouped together so that visitors can explore related phenomena in a variety of ways.

The Exploratorium uses gallery 'Explainers', staff who can help explain to visitors the phenomena behind the exhibits. Artists and musicians have also collaborated in the development of exhibits.

If you can't make it to San Francisco, don't worry – you can almost certainly see some of the Exploratorium's work by visiting your nearest science centre. The *Exploratorium Cookbooks*, which provide guides to reproducing the most popular Exploratorium exhibits, have meant that Oppenheimer's vision has spread around the world.

The different approaches of science museums and science centres both have their pitfalls. Some would say science museums contain lots of technology but very little science; the material tools and products of science illustrate the business of science, but not the physical phenomena under investigation. Conversely, science centres have been criticized for presenting scientific phenomena as simple facts, without any context illustrating how our under-standing developed. Many institutions are now seeking to combine the best of both, by mixing media and layering information so that different interpret-ations can be provided.

Challenging times

The science communication boom of the 1990s brought good times for many science centres, but today's realities are harsher. In the United Kingdom a raft of new science centres opened as part of the Millennium Project, backed by lottery funding. While some, such as the Eden Project in Cornwall, were very successful, others have struggled. The Earth Centre in Doncaster and the Big Idea in Ayrshire have closed and @Bristol, the successor to the Exploratory, has been forced to close high-cost attractions such as its IMAX cinema. The Government took the position that it would not provide ongoing support for science centres which do not care for historic collections (museums do receive support, although this is eaten up by the huge cost of storing and maintain-ing collections). Science centres were therefore dependent on attracting large visitor numbers – which in turn helps attract sponsorship – to meet the high costs of running buildings and interactive exhibits. Centres in areas on the tourist trail have fared better than their counterparts in less-visited regions. Those that were dependent on visitors from their local catchment areas found that numbers tailed off quickly – most people will only visit an attraction once. Encouraging them to come back means changing exhibits regularly, which has major cost implications. In 2007 the House of Commons Science and Technology Committee published a report on *Funding of Science and Discovery Centres*, which suggested that the problem could be reduced by providing tax relief for science centres. As of the time of writing, this is still under review.

Although operating in a slightly less precarious environment, science museums are also facing financial challenges. As well as the building and exhibit maintenance costs faced by their science centre counterparts, museums also have to store and care for their collections. The growing gap between available funding and costs has led to the closure of some small museums, and cutbacks at large museums. Science museums and centres both have to compete with a large number of alternative visitor attractions. The challenge is for them to find ways to stay commercially viable without losing sight of their cultural and educational remits.

The very nature of the cultural remit is under discussion in many science museums. It is no longer practically possible to keep up with the vast pace of change in science, technology and medicine, so collections will not provide an encyclopaedic overview for future historians. Curators must collect stra-tegically in areas they consider likely to remain important in the long term. As new objects are collected, some older collections will likely have to make way to ensure enough storage. There is a growing shift away from collecting type specimens towards collecting objects that could be used to tell stories in (physical or virtual) displays.

Rather than the traditional narratives of scientific progress, museum curators are increasingly turning to the academic disciplines of history of science and technology to portray science in a more critically sophisticated way. However, this can prove a bit much for audiences to take on board, as the experience of the Smithsonian shows.

BOX 7.2   CASE STUDY: STRIFE AT THE SMITHSONIAN

In the 1990s, exhibits at two of the Smithsonian Institution's national museums in Washington D.C. illustrated the difficulties of keeping different audiences happy. This is increasingly the case as curators seek to explore the social context of science and technology, rather than uncritically present a shrine to masterworks. Many events (in the past and present) can be interpreted from different points of view; every artefact can be used to tell a variety of stories. Increasingly, museum exhibits try to present several points of view and allow visitors to make up their own minds. However, this can lead to clashes with those fixed in particular points of view.

Opening in 1994, *Science in American Life* was produced by the National Museum of American History and supported by a grant from the American Chemical Society. The exhibition team eschewed the traditional 'eureka moments' or 'great American scientists' approaches in favour of showing examples of the interaction between science and society, and how this affected American attitudes towards progress. The 22 case studies, illustrated by a mix of media, explore the complex relationships between science, technology and progress, for good and bad; stories covered include the Manhattan Project, the development of the birth control pill, and early cloning techniques. Lead curator Art Molella and his team took the premise that 'it is important for all Americans – scientists and non-scientists alike – to understand science as a responsibility of citizenship in a society increasingly dependent on science and technology'.

After opening, the exhibition came in for criticism from the scientific community, led by the American Physical Society. Science in American Life was criticized for placing too much emphasis on the downsides of science and not enough on its achievements; the debate was played out against the backdrop of the Science Wars (see Chapter 1). The Smithsonian countered with audience evaluation showing that visitors generally did not waver from their already positive perception of science after visiting the exhibition. However, the American Chemical Society expressed its dissatisfaction with the exhibition and declined to fund future developments. *Science in American Life* remains on display (although at the time of writing the museum is closed for major refurbishment), and Molella rose to a senior position in the Smithsonian.

Even more controversial was a proposed exhibit at the Smithsonian's National Air and Space Museum, featuring the *Enola Gay*, the plane which dropped the atomic bomb on Hiroshima. The exhibition's initial title, *The Crossroads: the End of World War II, the Atomic Bomb and the Origins of the Cold War* suggests its scope. The aim was to provide balanced coverage of the decision to drop the bomb, including testimony from a variety of sources, including historians, war veterans, eye-witnesses and survivors.

The exhibition team came under heavy pressure from the Air Force Association to improve the balance of coverage (in the AFA's eyes); for example it was suggested that emotive displays of the consequences of the Bomb, such as that of a child's lunch box retrieved from Hiroshima, should be counterpointed by coverage of Japanese atrocities in prisoner-of-war camps. The dispute shows that artefacts of science and technology are not simply symbols of progress but carry all manner of political, historical and moral baggage. The matter reached the mass media and eventually Museum director Martin Harwit was forced to resign.

In the end, it was impossible to find an interpretation that was deemed 'balanced' by all parties. The Crossroads exhibition was shelved. The *Enola Gay*'s fuselage eventually made it on display in 1995, but with only minimal interpretation.

Creating an exhibition

First principles

Know what you want to say
First of all, be clear why you're doing this exhibition and what you want it to say. If you don't define the scope then you are liable to end up with a mass of exhibits that are only vaguely related to each other, confusing for the visitor to navigate and with no particular outcome. Before you have started even thinking about what individual exhibits might look like, you should have done enough research into the subject area and available assets such as objects, pictorial material, multimedia etc., to identify the strongest angle for the exhibition. In many ways it's like pitching a feature to a magazine – if you can't sum up the main point in one sentence, then you don't have a story. Or, if you've got a fantastic story but no three-dimensional material to tell it with, then you haven't got an exhibition, you've got an article, book or film.

Scoping your exhibition gives you a clearer idea of what's in and what's out. You might have access to a rare and beautiful object, or a really fun computer interactive, but if they don't fit with your brief then there is no reason to include them. If you've stumbled across a must-have exhibit and it's early enough in the day, you may be able to go back to the drawing board and come up with a new angle that allows you to encompass all desired exhibits. Usually, you're not so lucky with timing, so you have to be ruthless.

Remember your exhibit may have to last quite a long time – both in terms of physical robustness, and content. Temporary exhibitions can last for anything from a few weeks to over a year. Permanent galleries are usually envisaged with a lifetime of around 10–15 years, although if opportunities to update or replace it don't materialize, you may find your gallery will still be there when your grandchildren come to visit. Walking through most large museums, containing galleries of different ages, you will find they are themselves a monument to changing fashions in museum design, from rows of glass cases, to dioramas and room sets, to hands-on displays and increasing use of multimedia technology. The particular curse of science museums is that the content is liable to become dated quite quickly. Some galleries are designed to be updateable but this is expensive and time-consuming so not possible in all cases. This means you'll have to plan your content, and the means of delivering it, carefully so it doesn't look hopelessly out of date before too long.

Know who you're saying it to

Choose your audience. If an exhibit is designed for 'everyone', it will end up pleasing no-one. Different visitors have different needs and expectations and will bring varying amounts of prior knowledge with them. You need to choose who your exhibition is primarily aimed at, tailor the delivery to them, and be clear in your marketing material so that people know what to expect.

For science museums and science centres, audiences tend to fall into three main categories:

- **Family groups:** The visit is usually led by the demands of the children. Parents find themselves viewing exhibits through their children's eyes and help to mediate the content for them. You should break this down further according to the age of the children.
- **School groups:** Teachers want content relevant (although not identical) to the school curriculum, which is broken down according to age group.
- **Adults visiting without children:** This is a broad group encompassing a wide age range, and spectrum of possible prior knowledge, so depending on the size of your exhibition you may want to pick a particular niche.

Make sure that your exhibition angle and your target audience match. If one of these has already been set, then tailor the other accordingly. If you are doing an exhibition about general relativity and under pressure to pitch it for school groups, point out to your bosses that the detailed physics content is way beyond the school curriculum. Similarly, if your brief is to design an exhibition about light for under fives and their parents, you might want to stick to shadow boxes and leave *New Insights into Newton's Corpuscular Theory* for another time.

For all but the smallest exhibitions, it is not practical to restrict your scope to a very narrow target audience: given the time and money that goes into creating museum exhibits, you want them to attract as many people as possible, and ideally you want to attract people who might not have bothered visiting your museum before now. This inevitably means that your visitors will have a range of backgrounds, knowledge and preferred learning styles. Choosing your exhibition media and interpretation strategies carefully will help each person to get the most from their visit.

It is important to realize that you are not creating an exhibit for yourself, and to keep the needs of visitors in mind at all times. Bear in mind that by the time they have reached your exhibition, visitors may have had to travel a long way to get to your venue; they have had to work out how to navigate the building; they may have had to face a long queue for the toilets, or deal with a truculent toddler. So to keep their attention, you need to make it easy for them to navigate the exhibition content, and offer them something fun.

Decide how to say it

The exhibition environment offers you an opportunity to appeal to people's different learning styles. Some people prefer to analyse information; others like to learn by trying things out; some like to learn by discussing with other people; most people will have a mix of preferences. Different exhibition media (text, objects, interactives etc.) can play to different learning styles. A rich exhibition will use a mix of different media, providing a multi-sensory experience, so that it has broad appeal for the different preferences of visitors.

Interpretation media

Working with objects

A museum's objects, and the stories of the people who made and used them, can be a powerful way of communicating science and its history. Visitors have a chance to see the 'real thing', often a unique artefact that can't be seen anywhere else. Objects can tell multiple stories with many meanings; they can mean different things to different people; but in many cases they don't speak for themselves, and you will need to help the visitor interpret them.

Some objects have a natural appeal: they're well known in their own right or associated with famous events, they're impressively large, they are striking or beautiful, they evoke feelings of nostalgia. Others need a bit more work. Unlike the collections in an art gallery, many of the objects that make up the collections in science museums were never meant to be seen in public; they were designed to perform a particular (sometimes obscure) function. It is not always obvious how a scientific instrument works, or even what it is. This can be a the case particularly with twentieth and twenty-first-century objects: the intricate brass and glass instruments of earlier centuries, which have immediate visual attraction even if their workings are harder to understand, have given way to anonymous grey boxes whose inner workings are completely hidden. You will need to help the visitor interpret them, with carefully written labels, or supporting videos and animations.

Displays tend to be object-led or story-led using the objects as illustration. Leading with objects means that the stories will be shaped around what objects are available. This may limit the range of available stories, but on the other hand can bring unique perspectives, and reveal stories that visitors can only encounter in the presence of the object. The story-led approach tends to prevail when dealing with contemporary science, where the content tends to be more issue-led. Objects can add an extra layer to the story telling, but it is important to ensure that they are carefully selected and interpreted so that visitors can see things in them that help tell the story, rather than just using them as props. The label text is important as it gives visitors clues about what to look for.

Working with text

First and foremost, remember: an exhibition is not a book on a wall. Some museum visitors will start at the beginning and read every piece of text in sequence. However, most will gravitate towards individual exhibits that appeal to them (for example, a striking object, or an interactive game) and will then read the text around it to try and find out more about it. They will then move on to the next thing that catches their eye, skipping over big chunks of the exhibition text.

So exhibition text should be designed not to tell a complete story, but to enable your exhibits to tell the story. It should help visitors identify what each exhibit is and why it is there, encouraging them look more closely at the things in front of them.

The general rules of science writing (as seen in Chapter 4, Writing Science) apply: keep it clear, be active rather than passive, use the inverted pyramid structure to ensure the most important information is readily available. In an exhibition, further guidelines apply:

- **Make it easy for your visitors:** Bear in mind that an exhibition environment can be a difficult reading environment: there are lots of other things to distract the reader, there might be noise from some exhibits, it could be crowded, visitors might be rushing to see as much as they can during their visit and not have much time to trawl through information. Use clear headings and break up text into manageable chunks so that people can quickly pick out what they need. Work with your exhibition designer to ensure that text is laid out so that it's easy to find and read from a distance.
- **Make each piece of text stand-alone:** Since you can't assume that your visitor will have read the rest of the text in your exhibition, write your text so they can get as much useful information as possible from reading just the one piece. Don't use jargon that relies on people having read explanatory text elsewhere, and don't refer them to exhibits on the other side of the room.
- **Encourage people to look at what's in front of them:** The whole point of going to an exhibition is seeing things you can't find elsewhere, so your text should refer to the exhibits and not just contain information that could be found in a book. Point out interesting things that visitors can look for – this is particularly useful for adults visiting with children. So, for example, rather than saying 'On re-entry the Apollo 10 spacecraft hit speeds exceeding 24790 mph, the fastest a crewed vehicle has ever travelled', say 'On the underside of the spacecraft you can see the scorch marks from its re-entry to Earth. It hit speeds of over 24790 mph, a record for a crewed vehicle'.

Your primary exhibition text will appear on wall panels and object labels. The need to keep things clear for visitors and pressure of space (designers like to keep things uncluttered, and text needs to be big enough for people to read) you are unlikely to have more than 50 to 60 word chunks to play with. It is therefore important that you get your essential information across succinctly.

For those who want to know more, you can provide further information in gallery books or computer stations. Make sure these provide relevant background detail to expand on the points in the main exhibition text, rather than being an information dump for all that interesting research you couldn't quite find room for in the main displays. Keep in mind the guidelines about reading in exhibitions: although you can include more detail here, it's still not an easy environment to take in lots of text. If you feel that you need to cover a lot of ground, you might want to provide seats so that people can take more time to read things through in comfort. Obviously, it would still be much easier for visitors to read things at home, so you may wish to provide leaflets to take away, provide additional exhibition information online, or point visitors towards sources of information beyond the exhibition.

Of course some people won't ever read *any* of the text you have slaved over, but that's visitors for you.

AV exhibits

Audio-visual exhibits add to the sensory experience of an exhibition and can help bring the displays to life. Interviews with key players or archive news footage highlight the human aspects of your story. Reconstructions or animations can help to illustrate the principles behind different scientific phenomena, or how particular objects on display work.

You need to bear in mind how a particular AV installation will fit in with the rest of the exhibition. Noise from an installation may be distracting in an area where people want to focus on looking at objects and labels; if noisy installations are too closely spaced they will interfere with each other. Using headphones means that only a small number of visitors can enjoy an exhibit at one time; they are okay for an exhibit providing extra information but not a good choice if the exhibit carries important content you want everyone to hear. Exhibition galleries are also noisy environments, so your exhibit soundtrack may be drowned out. It's wise to use subtitles to help people understand the message.

Audio guides are a fairly common way of allowing visitors to access additional information about individual exhibits that there has not been room for on the label. These can point out particular features of objects, provide further background information, or allow visitors to listen to relevant recordings. The downsides of audio guides are that they can discourage communication between visitors in groups, as everyone is busy listening at their own pace, and can cause crowding around exhibits as everyone stands there waiting for the soundtrack to finish.

Beware of making video or sound exhibits too long – visitors have a lot to see in the gallery and may not want to look/listen through a lengthy exhibit. As a rule of thumb, three minutes is the longest time the average visitor will spend at an AV exhibit before moving on to something else. If you must have something longer, it is a good idea to have this in a separate area with seating so that people have more comfort.

Interactive exhibits

Interactive exhibits, be they mechanical or computer-based, can be an excellent way to get visitors to actively engage with exhibition content rather than passively scanning information. However, they are expensive and time-consuming to create and maintain, so you need to be sure they are right for the job. Test prototypes during development to make sure they are reliable. Try them out on your target audience (as described later in this chapter) to make sure people use them as you expect.

A good interactive should have a clear goal and be simple to operate. Visitors tend to approach interactive exhibits like assembling flat-pack furniture: they ignore long instructions and just get stuck in. If you want them to pay attention to information, you need to build it into the experience so that they have to work through the information before progressing further. In a computer-based interactive this is relatively easy: you can program your exhibit so control buttons don't become active until the explanatory text has been on the screen for a short time. Getting visitors to work through instructions is harder to do with a mechanical interactive so it's best to avoid the need for complex instructions and make your exhibit as intuitive to operate as possible.

Your interactive should have a script – this describes what happens at each stage. It can be a written document, or a storyboard, and is the basis your software or hardware designers will use to build it. An interactive script should work through the challenge, the instructions needed, the different possible outcomes, and what can be learned from these. Even though your visitors are never going to see the script, it is useful for you to work it through. For more complex interactives, particularly computer-based ones, a flow chart can be useful to help you make sure that all possible outcomes make sense.

Your interactive should do more than just provide information at the touch of a button or the movement of a lever. That's not an interactive, that's just a dressed-up gallery book. There should be a challenge with different possible outcomes. This makes the visitor feel in control, and if you've done a good job they will be able to reflect on why different actions brought different results, reinforcing the learning points of your exhibition.

Visitors should have the option to work through the interactive a few times so that if they can't get it to work the first time, they can try again. Set the challenge appropriately to your target audience and the exhibition content: if it's too easy visitors will get bored, if it's too hard they will get frustrated.

Overall, the whole experience should not take too long to play through or people will abandon the activity before finishing. Ideal timescales depend on the nature of the task and the exhibition environment, but as a rule of thumb three minutes (as with AV exhibits) is the longest people will spend on a single go. Some people will stay much longer than this and play over and over again. Popular interactives can often have long queues so if space and budget allow you may want to provide more than one station.

Interactives can be multi-user, getting visitors to interact with each other. In some, visitors can play different roles and need to cooperate to achieve the final outcome. But you should remember that your visitor might be the only person in front of your exhibit on a quiet afternoon, or might just hate interacting with strangers, so it should be possible for one person to work an exhibit if required.

You will need to work with designers and software experts to ensure that the experience of working the interactive is suitable for your audience. Make the most of senses other than sight – touch, hearing and even smell can add to the experience (taste is usually best avoided, although the youngest visitors will have a tendency to lick your exhibits). Mechanical interactives should take into account different physical abilities – don't put controls four feet off the ground where they cannot be reached by children, or visitors using wheelchairs. When it comes to computer interactives, remember your younger visitors are probably much savvier than you are. You are unlikely to have the budget to compete with the hugely sophisticated graphic interfaces available on home gaming systems, so don't even try. As long as the content is fun and interesting, a fairly simple interface will still work. Older visitors may not be so confident at using computers, or have experience of playing games onscreen, so make sure that the controls are easy enough for an inexperienced user to understand and operate. Both mechanical and computer interactives suffer a lot of wear and tear so minimize fiddly or delicate controls that will need constant replacing.

BOX 7.3   CASE STUDY: REJUVENATING A MUSEUM

Until 2005 the municipal natural history collections of Winterthur in Switzerland were displayed in the fashion typical of early twentieth-century collections: ranks of objects including stuffed animals, geological specimens and relief maps, with little interpretation. They did not attract many visitors away from the art collections housed in the same building. A major refurbishment has changed the situation.

Rather than consign the bulk of the historic collection to storage, often an unfortunate side-effect of museum refurbishments, director Hans-Konrad Schmutz and his team made a conscious decision to work with the existing collection and interpret it in new ways. Their strategy was to ground the exotic collections in the familiar, making the displays relevant to the story of Winterthur itself and its inhabitants.

The display themes range from the flora and fauna found in and around a typical family house to the geological processes that created the Winterthur area. The exhibit sets are stark grey and white angular structures (for example a setting representing a house and garden), with the objects set amongst them, often at unexpected angles. This allows the objects to stand out, and the stuffed animals and birds seem alive again. Multimedia installations allow you to hear what different birds sound like; see how different flowers open at different times of the day; find out how animals become fossils. One room is a room-set of a merchant ship, exploring how the more exotic parts of the museum collection came to Winterthur. A children's space with storytelling and activities offers something for the youngest visitors.

The newly rechristened Naturmuseum Winterthur is now a lively and attractive space for family visitors, earning a nomination for 2007 European Museum of the Year.

Beyond the exhibition

Museums on the web

Museums and science centres are increasingly using their websites to extend and enhance their reach. While the website provides practical information that helps to make visits more enjoyable, like maps and information about where to eat and rest, it can also provide content. This could be material that supports and complements exhibitions at the museum, or content specially developed for the web. The website enables the museum's content to be accessed by people who can't physically reach the venue; the web can enhance the learning of visitors by offering utilities for before and after their visit.

It is important to treat the website as a separate entity from the exhibition, and not just duplicate the exhibition content online. You need to bear in mind that people use gallery spaces and web pages in different ways, and tailor the content for each accordingly. The web allows users to cross-link through different themes, lends itself well to visual and audio material, and allows you more room for additional information than you would have in an exhibition. It can provide a platform for user feedback, surveys and discussions, which are not always easy to provide in a gallery.

Having said that, the website should not end up being just the information dump for the stuff you couldn't fit in the gallery. It needs to be a self-contained experience in its own right. For example, the Science Museum's *Making the Modern World* website (http://www.makingthemodernworld.org. uk) launched in 2004 as a companion to the Museum's flagship gallery of the same name which opened in 2000. While it is based on the same chronological timelines as the gallery, and has pictures of the important objects on display at the Museum, the content is structured around different themes and guided tours and is designed as a series of rich media environments to make the most of audio, sound and zooming tools.

Many science museums have developed digital collections databases. While looking at a two-dimensional image on a computer is never going to compare with seeing the real thing in three dimensions, a digital database can give people an idea of the range of the museum's collection and be a useful tool for people trying to find out more about particular subject areas. It is also an approach to making public the stored collections – which can constitute upwards of 90 per cent of a large museum's collection. This can be particularly useful for specialist researchers. The Museum of the History of Science in Florence is usually completely unnoticed by the throngs queuing for the Uffizi Gallery around the corner, but holds several instruments made by Galileo (and, rather gruesomely, the embalmed middle finger of his right hand). The Galileo//Theka@ online database (accessible at http://www.imss.fi.it) allows the user to download information about the museum's holdings and resources elsewhere, including objects, books, reconstructions of experiments, and even itineraries for Galileo-related tours of Tuscany.

Many museums and science centres are now looking at incorporating more user-generated content into their websites, for example community-based online exhibitions, blogs, or opportunities to add to information about digitized collection objects. Institutions need to find a balance between allowing users to create their own content and maintaining the authoritative standards expected of museums and science centres, so at the moment most content is moderated by a staff member.

Several museums and science centres, such as the Exploratorium, are creating spaces in virtual worlds such as Second Life, where they can test exhibits that would be too difficult, expensive, or just too counter to the laws of physics to build in the real world. Some museums, such as the International Spaceflight Museum (accessible through Second Life), exist only virtually. Many of these activities are still at the experimental stage and it remains to be seen what kind of learning opportunities they offer the virtual visitor; an environment that is by nature entirely digital and cannot offer the 'real thing' experience of the physical museum, but it does offer lots of opportunity for community interaction. And virtual exhibits have begun to influence real ones: in 2008 The Tech Museum of Innovation in Silicon Valley launched an initiative inviting users to design exhibits for their Second Life presence. These were judged by an expert panel and the best were constructed in the real world museum.

Live interpretation

A major part of the interpretation in any science museum or science centre will be live presentations: gallery tours, drama, storytelling, demonstrations of working objects, live experiments etc. Event development and presentation techniques are described in more detail in Chapter 6, Presenting Science. Live events in the evening are a useful way of attracting the adult audience, particularly those who are put off visiting museum galleries by the thought of hordes of overexcited children. They can also provide a forum for covering topics that might not be suitable for the family and school audiences that make up the bulk of museum visitors. Several museums now have purpose-built adult event spaces, such as the Science Museum's Dana Centre and the Wellcome Collection in London.

Visitor reaction

You can create the most stunning, well-researched exhibition, but if nobody comes to see it, or those that do don't understand it, you have failed. Evaluating exhibitions can help you work out which aspects are successful and which aren't, so that you can tailor things better in future.

In the same way that you have to be clear about what your exhibition says and how you say it, you must be clear about what your evaluation is asking, and tailor the study accordingly. If you want quantitative evidence (e.g., what percentage of exhibition visitors are female; average length of stay in the gallery) you will need to sample a large number of people to be statistically reliable. If you are looking for more qualitative evidence (e.g., whether visitors understand an interactive exhibit; what views visitors hold about the topic being covered) then you will need to study people in greater depth, so your sample size is likely to be smaller. In both cases you should select your subjects carefully so that they represent a reasonable cross-section of the exhibition's target audience.

Asking the questions

The easiest, cheapest and least staff-intensive way to get visitor reaction is by providing feedback forms or visitor books for people to fill out at their leisure. However the information you can glean from these tends to be almost worthless. Most people won't have the time or inclination to fill out questionnaires at the end of a visit. Unfortunately, human nature being what it is, people don't often make an effort to praise, but do so to complain. So you are likely to end up with a negatively skewed response. If you've got teenagers visiting, you'll probably also get a lot of obscene scrawls.

You will get more useful results from interviewing visitors on (the?) gallery. Just asking people 'what did you think' will not give you answers that you can compare across the board, so you need to have a pre-planned questionnaire that quickly allows you to extract useful information. Introduce yourself to your chosen visitor(s) and tell them that you'll only take five minutes of their time – they will relax once they know you are not going to box them in for half an hour. It's usually a good idea to tell them that you didn't work on the exhibition (even if that isn't true), as they will speak more freely if they are not afraid of hurting your feelings. A mix of open and closed questions is generally the most useful way to glean information.

Open-ended questions will allow visitors to volunteer information, for example,

■   What do you think this exhibit was about?
■   Was there anything you particularly liked?
■   Was there anything you didn't enjoy?
■   Is there anything you think we could do to improve this exhibition?

You may need to gently prompt visitors to draw out more responses – try and rephrase your question, or ask what they thought about particular aspects. If they still can't give you a detailed answer, don't pressure them. Don't rush through the questions – if you stay quiet, people will be more likely to come out with more information to fill the silence.

Closed questions are useful for quantitative analysis, as they limit the range of possible responses, for example,

■   How would you rate this exhibit: very good/good/okay/poor/not sure
■   Can you select the words from this list that reflect how you feel about this exhibit: boring/interesting/entertaining/confusing/fun/none of the above

Avoid:

■   Loaded questions – How do you think this new exhibit has improved the gallery?
■   Questions that require a lot of background knowledge – Do you think this exhibition accurately reflects the current state of stem cell research?
■   Quizzing your visitors on the detailed content of the exhibition text – Evaluation is not an exam.

Observing visitors

Watching how your visitors behave in your exhibition can help you to work out how they use the space, identify popular and underused exhibits, and how they interact with particular exhibits.

When looking at the overall exhibition, use a gallery map on which you track the movement of individual visitors. Things to watch out for are:

■   What route do they take around the exhibition?
■   What exhibits do they look at? Do they notice exhibits or signage overhead?
■   How long do they spend at particular exhibits?

■ How do they interact with exhibits – do they read text, do they touch, do they point?

■ Do they interact with other visitors, or museum staff?

You might want to observe particular exhibits closely and have a list of specific things to look out for. When studying a computer interactive, you might want to track whether visitors work out the control buttons, read through the text and play through more than once.

Observation, without the support of a questionnaire, will tell you *how* visitors behave, but not *why*. You can't assume that visitors really engaged with a particular exhibit just because they spent ages in front of it. They might have been baffled and spent ages trying to work out what it was about. A particular gallery might seem very popular because it happens to be on a busy through route; another might be empty not because its content is unpopular, but because it's out of the way and badly signposted.

BOX 7.4   CASE STUDY: *WHO AM I?* AT THE SCIENCE MUSEUM

Who am I?, part of the Science Museum's Wellcome Wing suite of contemporary science galleries, covers genetics and brain science. It opened in 2000 and takes as its theme how modern science is changing our perception of what it means to be human. Interpretation is delivered via object displays, computer interactives and artworks interspersed among the objects.

The gallery has benefited from front-end (at the outset) formative (carried out during gallery development) and summative (carried out after opening) evaluation. During the gallery development the team carried out a series of visitor focus groups with people from different age groups. The feedback was that a gallery about genetics would be difficult to understand, and visitors found it difficult to imagine the types of exhibits that the gallery might contain. The feedback helped to steer the gallery team towards an approach which took as its starting point something everyone was familiar with: themselves. Questions, such as 'where do you get your looks from?, 'did we all come from Africa?, and 'how do you know so much?' grounded new developments in genetics and brain science in the personal.

The summative evaluation found that this approach was successful. Over a period of several months, the evaluation team surveyed hundreds of visitors using a number of approaches: tracking randomly selected visitors, conducting exit interviews, focus groups and closely accompanied visits. Visitors responded positively to the exhibition, with the majority able to identify what the gallery's key learning points were and describing the experience as entertaining, educational and informative. The evaluation helped to identify elements that were not working so well, such as labelling of the artworks (many were missed by visitors) and orientation. *Who am I?* is due for a major renewal, to reopen 2010, and will use results from this evaluation and other studies to ensure the second-generation gallery builds on the success of the first.

Whatever type of evaluation methods you adopt, ensure that it is not an empty exercise. The recommendations from the evaluation should be followed through. If trials of a prototype exhibit show that it's not working for visitors, it needs to be changed or abandoned, even if that means you have to change things you personally like. There is not always enough funding left to make major changes to galleries once they have opened, but if you can't change unsuccessful exhibits at least make sure that the learnings from the evaluation feed into your next project.

Conclusion

Exhibiting science is not an exact art. These are general guidelines, but it takes flair to pull off something really memorable. The best thing to do is to visit as many museums and science centres as you can, to get a feel for the kinds of things that work with visitors, and to get inspiration.

One of the great things about working in exhibitions is that you get to see firsthand how your audience interacts with your finished product, in a way that you can't with writing or broadcasting. If you get it right, it's incredibly rewarding to see people enjoying what you've built. If you get it wrong, at least you've learned for next time.

ACTIVITIES

▪ Take an ordinary household item and write a museum label about it. Try writing different versions pitched for different target audiences.

▪ Storyboard an interactive exhibit based on a scientific concept of your choice. remember to specify a target audience.

▪ Keep a journal comparing your visits to different museums and science centres: what approch do they take? How do other visitors seem to react to the display?

▪ Why not volunteer at your nearest museum or science centre? Many institutions have volunteer schemes offering a range of roles. It's a great way to get real experience.

References and further reading

Butler, Stella. (1992), *Science and Technology Museums*, Leicester University Press (Leicester).

Durant, John, (ed.) (1992), *Museums and the Public Understanding of Science,* Science Museum (London).

Gammon, Ben. (2003), *Assessing Learning in the Museum Environment: A Practical Guide for Museum Evaluators*. Available online from http://www.ecsite-uk.net/events/reports/indicators_learning_1103_gammon.pdf (accessed April 2008).

* MacDonald, Sharon. (ed.) (1997), *The Politics of Display: Museums, Science, Culture*. Routledge (London).

Molella, Arthur and Stephens, Carlene. (1996), Science and Its Stakeholders: The Making of 'Science in American Life', in Pearce, Susan M. (ed.), *Exploring Science in Museums*, The Athlone Press.

* indicates a more difficult read for the undergraduate reader (although note most of these works are aimed at museum peers or postgraduate researchers).

Useful web links

Association of Science & Technology Centers: http://www.astc.org/
European Network of Science Centres and Museums: http://www.ecsite.net
Museums Association: http://www.museumsassociation.org/
Museums and the Web: http://www.archimuse.com/conferences/mw.html
Natural History Museum: Winterthur: http://www.natur.winterthur.ch (in German)
The Science Museum: http://www.sciencemuseum.org.uk

Index